Behavioral Finance

Behavioral Finance

Joachim Goldberg and Rüdiger von Nitzsch

Translated by
Adriana Morris

JOHN WILEY & SONS, LTD
Chichester • New York • Weinheim • Brisbane • Singapore • Toronto

First published in German under the title *Behavioral Finance* by FinanzBuch Verlag GmbH.

Copyright © 1999 FinanzBuch Verlag GmbH

English edition published in 2001 by   John Wiley & Sons Ltd,
Baffins Lane, Chichester,
West Sussex PO19 1UD, England

National   01243 779777
International (+44) 1243 779777
e-mail (for orders and customer service enquiries):
cs-books@wiley.co.uk
Visit our Home Page on http://www.wiley.co.uk

Translated from German by Adriana Morris

English translation © 2001 John Wiley & Sons Ltd

Reprinted February 2002

Other Wiley Editorial Offices

John Wiley & Sons, Inc., 605 Third Avenue,
New York, NY 10158-0012, USA

Wiley-VCH Verlag GmbH, Pappelallee 3,
D-69469 Weinheim, Germany

John Wiley & Sons, Australia Ltd, 33 Park Road, Milton,
Queensland 4064, Australia

John Wiley & Sons (Asia) Pte Ltd, 2 Clementi Loop #02-01
Jin Xing Distripark, Singapore 129809

John Wiley & Sons (Canada) Ltd, 22 Worcester Road,
Rexdale, Ontario M9W 1L1, Canada

Library of Congress Cataloging-in-Publication Data

Goldberg, Joachim, 1956–
Behavioral finance/Joachim Goldberg and Rüdiger von Nitzsch,
    p. cm.
Includes bibliographical references and index.
ISBN 0–471–49784–3 (cloth : alk. paper)
1. Investments—Psychological aspects. 2. Investments—Decision making. 1. Nitzsch, Rüdiger von. II. Title.
HG4515.15.15 .G65 2001
332.6—dc21   00–047750

British Library Cataloguing in Publication Data

A catalogue record for this book is available from the British Library

ISBN 0–471–49784–3

Typeset in Times Ten and Bauer Bodoni by Footnote Graphics, Warminster, Wilts.
Printed and bound in Great Britain by Biddles Ltd, Guildford and King's Lynn

This book is printed on acid-free paper responsibly manufactured from sustainable forestry, in which at least two trees are planted for each one used for paper production.

Contents

Preface

People don't like lottery or raffle tickets bearing the number 1. On the one hand, reason tells us that it could win us the 12,000 dollars just as well as any other ticket; on the other hand, we can hear an inner voice exhorting us not to take it, for who has ever heard of such a small number winning a large prize?

Georg Lichtenberg (1776–1779) described the classic situation of making a decision under conditions of uncertainty very well with this aphorism. The voice of reason does not always win through in this situation, even when we can calculate probability and know very well that lottery ticket number 1 is as likely to win as any other number. At the same time, there is another, quieter voice that appeals to our secret fears and longings. And we usually listen to the latter.

What exactly is this powerful *Je ne sais quoi* that Lichtenberg refers to? For years, nobody tried to find an answer to this question; we prefer to ignore the existence of something of which we cannot speak. The world of finance has always been an area of pure rationality, where only one god is worshipped, namely profit.

Where does the mass euphoria come from? Why do speculation bubbles burst, causing panic selling? Why are markets so unpredictable, and why do prices not move as expected? These questions continued to vex one of the authors of this book. As a typical trader, he became interested in the practice of chart analysis, a branch of technical analysis. This was more than 15 years ago. In the beginning, he tried only to guess the imminent movement of prices from the tangle of lines and figures as displayed by charts. Technical analysis theory implies that these patterns reflect the behavior of actors and therefore disclose the future behavior of buyers and sellers. Some scientists regard this as being subjective and hardly an improvement on reading tea leaves; others criticize it as purely self-fulfilling prophecy.

The author soon realized that technical analysis could not offer satisfactory answers to his questions. The scientific basis for this method seemed too uncertain and too vague. He therefore began to study what seemed to him fundamental to market developments, based on his daily observations: the thoughts and emotions of the people who participated in the markets. He came to the conclusion that the source of all success and failure lies in the human brain – a bold conclusion. Nevertheless, he owes the theory of the three basic human types to his intensive study of the physiology of the human brain and behavioral biology. Yet market developments could still not be predicted on the basis of these findings.

A lecture given by the author to students at the Aachen University of Technology in Germany, and more precisely the present that one of the attendees gave him, provided the breakthrough. This present was a dissertation on prospect theory developed by Kahneman and Tversky as an incentive for further research, and he was extremely interested in the findings from numerous experiments on human decision making conducted by the two American scientists. It put the work he had done in an entirely different perspective; at last he seemed to have found the key with which to unlock the secrets of the market.

Shortly after, he met the professor who supervised the dissertation. This scientist had been studying the subject of decision making for some time. He was particularly interested in the question as to how people could make sensible (rational) decisions if the issue was very complex and multifaceted. He enjoyed designing models and instruments that might prove to be suitable tools. But the decision-making theorist subsequently realized that mathematical models and rationality axioms offer an insight into human psychology, rather than aiding decision making. Ultimately, irrational decisions are governed by particular behavior patterns, which have a psychological basis, rather than a lack of technical tools. This realization finally led him to study prospect theory in detail. He was impressed by its substance and elegance.

Whether a decision is rational or not is very clear when money is concerned. Against this background, meeting a like-minded, interested and experienced insider from the world of finance proved to be a happy event for the scientist. There were many discussions. The encounter between theory (understanding) and practice (experience) proved extremely productive, confirming Kant's statement that understanding without experience remains as empty as experience without understanding is blind. Much of what until then could be grasped only intuitively, or merely suspected, suddenly became clear and transparent – gray theory took on colour and came alive.

The term "behavioral finance" covers a new branch of capital market analysis born some years ago in the USA. Here, the disciplines of economics and psychology meet. The new discipline has proved to be very fruitful, and findings and ideas are also now adopted in Europe. The subject is enjoying a growing popularity in Germany. We are of the opinion that we can lift some of the fog around this new scientific as well as practical discipline, not least on the basis of the comprehensive interaction between theory and practice developed by us. We decided to commit our thoughts to paper, hence this book.

Like many other publications, this book does not claim to be comprehensive. Behavioral finance is a young and growing area of research, which is subject to ongoing change and new aspects, and which ultimately always leads back to the original principles. Three years is a long time, and we have to end somewhere, knowing that we have not yet examined all aspects of human behavior, only the most important ones. At the very least, we hope to have shown the financial markets from a point of view that renders them less mystical and therefore more human. Ultimately, a market is only a meeting point for people who wish to exchange goods or information.

We would like to express our thanks for the abundant support that we received. In particular, we thank Christian Friedrich who has worked closely with us throughout this book, and enhanced it with clever suggestions. He was always ready to offer constructive criticism if we went off-target. A special thankyou to our wives, who accepted, with humour, that the communication between Aachen and Frankfurt via email eventually exceeded communication with each of them personally. We would especially like to thank Barbara Goldberg who, as a skilled journalist, polished up our manuscript. We also owe a thankyou to Christian Freidrich's girlfriend, Kristina Janssen, who wrote the dissertation referred to above, which ultimately brought us together.

Finally, we would like to thank Paul D. MacLean who developed the theory of the triune brain, and who willingly put a collection of his most important essays and work at out disposal. And last but not least, we thank Guido Kiell of the University of Cologne for his encouragement.

September 1999
Joachim Goldberg
Rüdiger von Nitzsch

Chapter 1

Forecasts

Fundamentals, technical analysis and behavioral finance

Many people wish to look into the future and know what is going to happen. They do not like surprises sprung on them by fate or by other people; they prefer to be in control of their own destinies, and sometimes other people's destinies as well. Predictions of one kind or another have been popular from the beginning of civilization, particularly where far-reaching and difficult decisions are involved. Remember the prophets of the Old Testament, the Oracle at Delphi, the Sibylline Oracles, and astrology, practiced for thousands of years? Such authorities would often be consulted when the future looked uncertain.

Forecasts relating to future price trends of, for example, stocks and shares, currency prices, and commodities are sought after by those trading in the financial markets so they can take positions that yield most profit within the shortest possible time. Forecasts have become the be all and end all of the financial markets. Without them, many a player would lack the necessary imagination in respect of future developments and commitments in the markets, as well as the necessary confidence in the form of a supposed guarantee to be able to shape at least part of their own future.

Well-founded forecasts are difficult to compile, and many people consider it impossible to make sound predictions for the long term. That does not prevent a whole host of analysts all over the world from trading in a product called "the future". Their job is to compile forecasts. Analysts who get it right think that they are better than others and believe they can therefore also indirectly control what happens in the markets. This often proves to be an illusion.

The motivation for acting on forecasts lies not only in the quest for the greatest possible gains, or in insurance against unfavorable market developments. People would prefer to eliminate any uncertainty as to whether a particular decision will lead to success. The bottom line is not just a positive material result, for to many people appearing clever means at least as much as a small gain.

The success or otherwise of forecasts is very difficult to measure. The popular prediction that the dollar will reach point x in 12 months' time may well turn out to be true, but the crux for the market participant is how the currency gets to point x. People will normally discover this only if they themselves have "traded" on the forecast in question, in other words they have entered into a commitment. That is when they discover that prices don't move in a straight line over the forecast period, and that movements are, for the most part, irregular. Investment losses in the short term can exert psychological pressure on market participants to the extent that they are forced to give up midway, i.e. they liquidate their position. To add insult to injury, a year later they then read the following phrase in investment letters: "As we said 12 months ago, the dollar will stand at point x in a year's time." The forecast has come true. Unfulfilled predictions, however, are forgotten quickly. Nobody boasts about having been let down by a false prediction.

Professional analysts also tend to issue predictions in line with other analysts, and even to deliberately match their predictions to those of their colleagues. This makes it more or less unlikely for an individual analyst to be rejected by his or her band of followers, as no one upsets the general harmony by offering a contrary opinion. The outsider tip, on the other hand, causes a greater stir. If the tip is successful, then the forecaster's reputation is made, particularly as a beginner; if not, then it doesn't matter, because the forecast was not based on realistic assumptions anyway, and only ever had a very small chance of coming true.

Directional predictions (rises and falls) are useless if we do not know by how much the price of the commodity will change. The likelihood of a hit is relatively great if the extent of the predicted movement is only small. But what happens if the direction of the movement is wrong? Market participants are left high and dry just when it becomes clear that a forecast might be wrong – they often do not know which market factors will render a forecast useless. Only those who acted on the forecast and subsequently suffered a loss will be made aware of them.

So, analysts are under pressure to perform: they must be right as often as possible, and their forecasts must show a high hit rate. Yet more than anything, forecasts must sell well, which is why analysts often resort to vague predictions. The prediction of an event, for instance, is often accompanied by a probability score. Take the prediction that the Central Bank will raise the bank rate at its next meeting, with a probability score of 70 per cent, which gives the impression of a worthwhile prediction but contains a high degree of uncertainty if you remember that odds of 50:50 are in fact completely useless. Scores of 90 or 10 per cent, on the other hand, are hardly ever offered by analysts in these investment letters.

The recommendation to buy share x at a price that lies between 40 and 45 euros, accompanied by a short-term target yield of 110 euros, must be regarded as a vague recommendation. Even if the shares could be bought at 45 euros only, and possibly also only in small quantities, then the originator of this forecast will still assume, mostly wrongly, that all buy orders can be executed at 45 euros. This typically happens when the analyst does not have any experience of trading or is not close to the market. Of course, people are pleased when the share price subsequently rises to 110 euros as predicted. But who, apart from the analyst, whose reputation is enhanced, can profit from such recommendations if no one is selling?

Until barely two decades ago, and particularly in Europe, the study of the markets and the various factors that influence them used to be confined to a branch of economics – fundamental analysis – which studies the influence of economic facts and trends on market developments. The broader field includes research into, and evaluation of, political events, for these affect the prices of stocks and shares, currencies prices, interest rates and other commodities. An essential condition for the practice of fundamental analysis is that participants in markets evaluate data and findings rationally, and make consistent use of them.

Critics of fundamental analysis accuse it of not being flexible enough to take into consideration unexpected changes in economic factors surrounding the markets before it is too late, as the effects of economic and political facts often kick in after a delay that cannot be predicted. Actors in financial markets are therefore frequently faced with timing problems when entering positions (Goldberg 1990).

The evaluation of economic data, moreover, often demands considerable knowledge, which cannot be presumed to be present to the same extent in all market participants. In addition, competition between the different economic schools often leads to ambiguous results in market analyses or forecasts. Nevertheless, fundamental analysis enjoys considerable popularity as far as medium- and long-term forecasts are concerned (6–12 months or longer), because it identifies the reasons why markets have developed in a particular direction. It is often used as a basis, if not a justification, for individual trading decisions. However, investors should not disregard knowledge of economic laws, as economic events can often trigger considerable price movements in the markets. In other words, fundamental analysis is certainly useful for long-term purposes.

It only becomes problematic when future developments need to be quantified. What is the use, for instance, of a forecast that the US dollar will be quoted three per cent higher against the euro than is currently the case, if the price subsequently falls by ten per cent and only later rises in line with the original prediction? The main drawback of such a prediction lies in the fact that currency prices cannot be controlled in the meantime, even if the hit rate remains consistently high in the long term, and they may vary considerably from the predicted movement. This means that patience is needed when acting on fundamental forecasts, which then conflicts with the objective of market participants to achieve the highest possible gain in the shortest possible time. Even highly successful forecasts are always accompanied by a high degree of uncertainty as to whether the prediction will come true.

Market participants who have large volumes to trade, on the other hand, often make use of price movements that set in shortly after the publication of fundamental data, in order to change their positions as discreetly as possible. This allows them to supply the market with liquidity where it would normally not be expected. Suppose, for example, that the price of the dollar is set to rise considerably against the euro following publication of surprisingly favorable fundamental data for the dollar. The rise is then subsequently dampened by people selling large trading volumes, as sufficient demand can only be found in precisely such a situation. The volume offered would depress the price if there was insufficient demand, so they have to follow the market. Something similar takes place when the price is set to fall following publication of data considerably worse than expected by the actors. The supply created will often be absorbed surreptitiously by the demand on the part of large market participants. Is it surprising then that markets do not behave fundamentally or rationally?

Participants in the various markets have increasingly made use of technical analysis over the past decade in order to compensate for the weaknesses of fundamental analysis as applied to short-term analyses. Technical analysis offers an array of useful instruments to identify trends early, and allows participants to respond flexibly to new events in the market. The only prerequisite for success in technical analysis is that demand and supply in a market must be able to develop more or less freely. Price developments cannot be interpreted meaningfully without this condition, as they would reflect information and opinions incompletely. The more prices are forced into a corset of narrow bands, as was the case, for instance, with the currencies in the European Monetary Union, the less they reflect the outcome of the process of information and opinion forming. Any lack of supply or demand in such cases will be masked by interventions and subventions. An extreme example is prices dictated by government, for example rigid exchange rates. In addition, the philosophy of technical analysis essentially rests on three premises.

The market price as a result of demand and supply contains all information and opinions that are available, whether rational or otherwise. This means that a price must also reflect all past and current economic data and political developments. Technical analysis has, in this respect, a real advantage over fundamental analysis: it can also respond to data and information evidently interpreted "wrongly", while fundamentally oriented market participants expect the market price to strictly obey the logic of economic data, which often entices them to continue to expect certain scenarios, even after price movements have indicated differently and losses have already been incurred. Technical analysis, on the other hand, is able to recognize early signs of a distortion of the market equilibrium. This is regularly the case when the limits of consolidation ranges are clearly breached. In such a situation, only the fact that one or more sellers or buyers have obviously responded, possibly on the basis of new information, is relevant. The reasons are not questioned. Finally, technical analysis tries to base predictions on historic events, i.e. on the basis of previous transactions and cash prices. It also tries to predict the robustness of future trends on the basis of consolidation zones, as they prevail, e.g. on the currency markets for 70 per cent of the time.

The second premise relates to prices moving in trends. The main purpose of technical analysis is to identify and make use of trends. Most of the successful technical trading models are based on following trends.

The third premise in technical analysis is that (market) history repeats itself. This might seem questionable, or at least worthy of discussion from a philosophical point of view. It is, in fact, based essentially on the assumption that prices and their movements reflect not only the interpretation of information and opinions, but also the behavior of actors participating in price formation. No one would seriously deny that human drives and passions, despite the general belief in progress, have changed little over the centuries. Technical analysis relies on consistency in human behavior by creating graphic records of price trends – charts – and looking for patterns that repeat themselves. Configurations depicted in the charts reflect the strength of demand and supply at a particular moment in time. These configurations are ultimately created by market participants through price formation, and they have a tendency to repeat themselves over time – just like the behavior of actors under particular life and market conditions, which is subject to logic and to a greater extent psychological mechanisms. All people, including market participants, react similarly in certain situations or under certain market conditions (e.g. stress). As long as the psychological constitution of the human mind remains essentially the same, the actions of market participants in relation to specific price developments will not change significantly (Goldberg 1990).

Technical analysis has readily attracted attention and recognition over the past five to ten years as an instrument for assessing short-term market developments (with a time horizon of up to three months), while long-term forecasts remain the province of economically oriented analysts. One reason for this differentiation could be increasing transparency in the markets. Thanks to modern media, information is now published so speedily that its contribution to price formation is minimal, as it becomes impossible for anyone to process the flood of incoming messages within a reasonable time span. Attempts to separate the wheat from the chaff in respect of reports arriving every second are bound to fail, as processing news under pressure of continuously and rapidly changing market situations can only take place superficially, as a reflex, if not more or less unconsciously.

Technical analysis has profited from the fact that market participants are overwhelmed by the quantity of information. It deals only with the observation of prices and their interpretation, which is why many people believe that it is an instrument that is simple to learn and use. Even though the price of a commodity reflects only part of all available information, it still portrays the opinions of sellers and buyers, which presently can also be technical. Chart points based on the study of configurations currently represent information, which is just as important as fundamental data. Some fundamental analysts even incorporate the main technical price levels in their analysis because you can't do without. But this leads to a false picture of the markets, because fundamental data and all expectations and opinions, whether correct or not, are already reflected in the market prices. Thus analysis feeds on itself (Goldberg 1997).

Unsubstantiated market reports used to spread slowly and gave market participants the feeling of being one step ahead of the competition. They now circulate so quickly that the use of possible information leads (excepting insider knowledge) fails, because most market participants receive the information at exactly the same time. Future charts produced by technical analysts will increasingly lack slowly-formed patterns; instead, they will be characterized by short, shock-type price developments. When most well-informed people wish to trade at the same time, then they will, by definition, not find enough counterparties on the other side.

Any clear-cut chart, on the other hand, is no longer a secret amongst a small conspiring community, ridiculed by the majority, but instead represents information that can be accessed by any professional market participant. The result is not a self-fulfilling prophecy, as critics of technical analysis purport, but a self-fulfilling destruction, so that only a few counterparties are available for people willing to trade on the by now dangerous and well-known chart points (similar to political or economic market information). There will be price jumps so large that the advantage that a technically oriented market participant has compared with other actors declines dramatically and an initially profitable transaction turns into a loss. Imagine the dollar reaching a high chart level, indicated for days as a buy recommendation by well-known information providers. Is it any wonder, then, that the majority of buyers cannot find sufficient selling capacity at this point, if they wish to act on the recommendation?

It can also happen that market participants intending to shift large volumes (say, after the publication of vital fundamental data) are waiting quite deliberately for high technical levels, in order to change their positions following publication. They might hold out against a large group of market participants who would like to buy dollars on the basis of a buy signal, i.e. they act as sellers, although this is contrary to expectation after a clear technical buy signal. And buyers are left to wonder why the price does not change, or even moves against their exposure.

Does that mean that technical analysis is finished? Not at all. But some of its instruments are decades old. Most importantly, various schools have been established for the (chart) technical interpretation of market developments. And many analysts have developed their own rules for the interpretation of configurations. The majority of analysts still swear by some kind of indicator (e.g. momentum lines, relative stress index (RSI), stochastics), which fools actors into believing that they can use them to control the market. Chart configurations, however, which are regarded by technical analysts as mirrors reflecting the conduct of market participants, are prevented from being realized almost by definition, due to their widespread availability. The failure to develop as predicted – the "false break" – has almost become the rule. But many technical analysts see what they expect and what they want to see.

Yet technical analysis, which is concerned with the recording of market prices and therefore of cash prices between buyers and sellers, is very appropriate for a successful capital market analysis. Its third premise – that market history repeats itself – is a small step in the right direction. Nevertheless, findings resulting from technical analysis remain superficial because it does not deal in sufficient detail with the human psyche, even though it is one of the essential factors in market transactions in the context of cash prices. Why is it then that actors are so often loath to sell shares that represent a loss? Why are people so much quicker to realize a profit? The things that actually motivate people are not taken into account sufficiently in these clever analyses; many scientists still regard the mind as largely unknown territory, others prefer to leave it alone, fearing it would amount to opening a Pandora's box.

Most fundamental analysts and economists refuse to get involved in the psychology of market participants. But technicians in particular should be concerned with human behavior, not only to calculate market movements, but also to understand them. A purely numerical study of prices, chart points and trend lines is far from sufficient to understand the markets. Analysts who neglect psychological factors cannot understand price developments, trading motives and the patterns on which they are based, and are therefore not able to analyze, let alone forecast, them adequately.

Participants in financial markets behave in various ways. Their motives, mentality, ways of thinking, willingness to accept risk and their trading horizons can be completely different. Although it is thought that actors act rationally, at least in their market dealings, reality shows a different picture: people act anything but rationally. Rationality from an economic point of view includes two essential characteristics (Schwartz 1998). Acting by market participants must be logical on the one hand, but on the other hand such action should lead to an increase in economic happiness. The latter is often not the case. People's motives for participation in the financial markets is not always maximization of profit. Such striving is considered to be totally immoral by some (mostly by those not participating, or by losers). Trivial motives, such as the quest for excitement and entertainment, entice many people to the stock exchange, while others are motivated by the desire for communication, or perhaps even common or garden jealousy. But motives influence and distort the way people perceive things.

Despite the intentions of many market participants to behave rationally, the outcome of their decisions often falls short of what could be considered optimal. They do their best but, like everybody else, they make mistakes. And these mistakes are repeated. This results in emotions, which may affect rational thinking and acting, and thus hamper rational decision making. In spite of this, followers of modern capital market theory still assume that market participants behave in a strictly rational manner. Although many actors are convinced that their actions are influenced by emotional factors, they do not believe that these elements can be quantified and that they occur systematically.

Fortunately, a new research field has been established over the past few years in the USA, which represents a behavior-oriented financial market theory – behavioral finance. This discipline is based on the fact that people act rationally only to a limited extent (De Bondt and Thaler 1995, Rapp 1997). In contrast to modern capital market theory, which attributes the pursuit of profit as the sole motive for trading by participants in financial markets, behavioral finance theory postulates that actors may have additional motives. It does not assume that market participants are fully informed. Actors do not always have access to important information, which may affect their decisions. Certain information may be unavailable, or may simply be missed or interpreted wrongly.

There is no doubt that people can absorb only so much information (Felser 1997). This restriction means that information must be selected and assessed according to its importance. Often, the selection process is based on irrational criteria, and errors may creep in. We know that different people evaluate the same information differently, reaching various, often completely opposite, conclusions. Studies and experiments in social psychology prove that people are always subject to misinterpretations and false conclusions when perceiving and processing information. These are not occasional "blips" compensated for by other "rational" market participants. On the contrary, anomalies and distortions occur systematically. And because they are systematic, conclusions as to future behavior on the part of market participants are feasible.

There are numerous examples of distortions of judgment. Yet many economic scientists assume rational action on the part of market participants, for instance, at times when large speculation bubbles occur, such as the "South Sea Bubble" in 1711 (Neal 1990). What led investors at the time to subscribe to shares in companies whose purpose, according to their articles of association, was to create something splendiferous, a company of whom nobody knew what it really produced? Market participants have clearly learnt nothing from Holland's tulipmania in 1634, except that the stock exchange crashes in 1929 and 1987 could have been prevented (Garber 1990), despite a much broader range of market instruments, considerably increased market transparency and transmission of information within seconds. The economist Richard Thaler, one of the fathers of behavioral finance, encapsulates it as follows: "If most individuals tend to err in the same direction, then a theory which assumes that they are rational also makes mistakes in predicting their behavior" (Thaler 1994).

Yet behavioral finance is concerned not only with the absorption and processing of information. It goes one step further and studies the decision-making behavior of participants in financial markets. Even when the alternatives seem completely clear, the way they are framed can influence the decision. But what happens when the choices are not so clear, when their realization depends on probability, which is usually difficult to quantify? Behavioral finance attempts to describe the actual, often intuitive behavior of decision makers, whether plausible or irrational, and to predict the behavior before, during and after a decision on this basis. This is relevant for the evaluation of behavior on the part of participants in capital markets in particular, as decision-making behavior that can be predicted is, in turn, of economic use to third parties. Actors who are aware of this type of behavior can identify their own errors in this context and learn to avoid them.

To portray the actions by market participants, and to predict future behavior on this basis, we must breathe life into the cold heart of *Homo oeconomicus* (to whom we will return later in greater detail). It follows that basic premises in psychology also apply to behavioral finance. These are mostly based on empirical research and experiments in decision-making behavior. Prospect theory, developed in the early 1980s by the psychologists Daniel Kahneman and Amos Tversky, represents an important milestone in this context. Kahneman and Tversky proved in numerous experiments that the day-to-day reality of decision makers varies from the assumptions held by economists.

Behavioral patterns that have traditionally been ignored by proponents of rational decisions are made transparent with the aid of prospect theory. These behavioral patterns arise because discipline and self-control are often overpowered by emotions and rendered ineffective. Moreover, people cannot oversee all the consequences of their actions (Bernstein 1996). Prospect theory and its findings – it has now been established as the main alternative to the classic expected utility theory (Levy 1997) – can be applied without difficulty to the behavior of participants in the financial markets. It helps to explain why actors in many decision-making situations act at best with "bounded rationality" (Simon 1955, Simon 1997).

But it does not stop with the analysis of trading decisions. The success or failure of a decision also affects future decisions, as we will see later. And not just this either. Information is regarded and evaluated differently in the light of a gain or the shadow of a loss. Cognitive dissonance theory (according to Festinger) is concerned with these phenomena and must therefore be included in behavioral finance, although the literature hardly touches on it.

Behavioral finance is concerned therefore with the absorption, selection and processing of information, and consequently with the resulting decisions. On the other hand, it also studies anomalies in human behavior. These deviations from rational acting are not limited only to exceptions, such as mass euphoria or panic reactions, which occur maybe once every decade: they are part of daily life and conduct. These actions, which are often not characterized by rationality, also affect other people, so that ultimately the interaction between market participants must also be studied.

One finding is that wrong interpretations and decisions can occur even if several people take part in opinion forming. Teams or colleagues do not always have a corrective effect. It is as well to deploy the methods and findings from social psychology for the study of group behavior.

Findings produced by behavioral finance must by definition also affect the field of technical analysis. Market participants continue to regard this as a kind of auxiliary science used for quantifying the results of fundamental analysis, i.e. translation into commercial chart points. Similarly, they do not afford technical analysis the status of a scientific analysis method; rather, they regard it as a kind of skill in the early identification of trends and trend changes. But that is exactly what makes it so vulnerable to criticism. Many of their younger proponents discover patterns that are not necessarily observed by others. Technical analysis is often successful only if, or even because, its forecasts are vague.

Technical analysis must therefore subject itself to a thorough revision if it is to remain credible, and some forecasting methods are likely to fall by the roadside. Technical analysis will basically only have a chance to survive in the long term if it is based on psychology, i.e. research findings in behavioral finance. That is where its strengths lie. This change is bound to take some time, as behavioral finance itself has not yet been fully developed in every area. Finally, technical analysis is an ideal tool to render behavior-oriented analysis of the capital markets useful for day-to-day trading.

Behavioral finance will therefore not only help improve one's own decision making, but will also contribute to a comprehensive understanding of actual behavior on the part of market participants. So far, this has been considered insufficiently by economists, as well as technicians. Readers will learn in the following chapters why they perhaps do not behave in an economically optimal and rational fashion. But those who understand the human mind might well obtain a clear lead compared with other actors, as they will be able to predict how most people will respond in particular situations. And because particular patterns of behavior are repeated again and again, they can also be predicted by third parties. And there is more: whoever is aware of these mechanisms could clearly increase their own trading success in the markets with the aid of a little discipline. The Delphi Oracle stated that the key to wisdom lies not in prediction of the future. In the language of the market, the success of a commitment is not based on clever forecasts alone. The advice to "know thyself" applies to modern market participants just as much as it did to the people of the ancient world.

Chapter 2

An analysis of exposure
Desire and reality

A description of fundamental and everyday experiences in the markets will help readers to understand the psyche of market participants and how it affects their behavior. To this purpose, a discussion of what is commonly called "mass psychology" will be less useful than a description of behavior that is commonplace. In other words, an experience in which readers can recognize themselves, at least partly. This description on its own could easily serve as an indication that rational behavior in financial markets should not be taken for granted.

This initial snapshot shows what happens in any currency-trading firm anywhere in the world. Something similar takes place in firms of brokers dealing in stocks and shares, commodities and many other markets. This section describes the behavior of a trader with a relatively short-term outlook, usually employed by a bank, who is permanently confronted with the task to end the trading day successfully, in other words to produce a profit from movements in the market. Not everyone will experience the pressure to perform to the same degree as this trader, but everybody should be able to recognize themselves at some stage in the following description. After all, anybody intent on participating in the financial markets wishes to avoid losses and to make large profits.

BETWEEN HOPE AND FEAR: PERSONAL EXPERIENCE

A trader is under pressure to perform as soon as his day starts. He uses a handheld device to access the latest currency prices and to follow further movements via satellite, so as to get a feel for the market. Ideally, he has studied the financial section of his newspaper in depth before arriving at his office in the morning, and he is already aware of the fundamental and political events relevant to the markets, and how these will affect prices. Discussions with colleagues and trading friends complete the picture, which will help form his opinion on short-term developments in relation to a currency, e.g. the euro versus the US dollar. Following intensive consultations, or merely acting on some vague feeling, the trader buys five million euros (a common unit of trading in the currency markets) in the expectation that the price will rise, preferably rapidly, so that he can subsequently sell them at a profit. Completing this transaction means that an idea on the part of the trader will become reality.

Hope soon turns into pleasure if the price moves as expected. This may grow into elation and exuberance, depending on the temperament of the trader. The open position is soon cleared, i.e. the profit created is realized, so as not to lose it again, and to avoid subsequent fears that the exposure might actually turn into a loss if the worst came to the worst. After all, he had been right in entering into this position in the first place, proving other people wrong, especially doubters. Material gain is added to the psychological satisfaction of having been proven right.

Success breeds confidence. A small but reassuring back-up fund is now available for the next commitment. The trader usually spends less time and effort on gathering information during this second round, as he basically already knows what he wants. The exchange of information with colleagues merely serves to confirm his personal opinion as regards price movements in the short term;

it is not a critical discussion with other experts. On the contrary, others tend to come to him for advice, so they would not normally contradict him.

The second trade is also successful, and the trader is very happy indeed. He is convinced he is in good form. Naturally, word of his success gets around; his colleagues need to, and must, back winners, and his opinion is in great demand. Unfortunately, objective information and interpretation are no longer required, and the trader acts on gut feeling alone. It seems as if the trader, spoiled by success, now has a compulsive need to repeat the feeling of happiness and recognition as often as possible. Increased confidence leads him to increase the size of his positions, with commensurate greater profits, which he hopes to realize as quickly as possible. He is already counting the profits for this month, minimizing or even disregarding losses. He now craves ever higher profits and recognition.

Three exposures – three hits. The week has started well. Trading volumes are raised once more, as such a run is not often seen. Although it does not work out so well this time ("At first the euro refused to move in my direction"), he still ends up with a profit, maybe even as large as last time. But the earlier profit was achieved with a small trading volume, i.e. with less risk. This slight blemish is best kept to himself or even suppressed – after all, only success counts. His happiness and increased zest for life reach a state of euphoria.

The never-ending calls from friends and colleagues are almost becoming a nuisance as the story of his golden touch spreads rapidly. A legend is created, even though we all know that such runs of luck do not last forever.

The successive emotional states of hope, joy, craving and euphoria, which can be observed in many successful market participants, distort their grasp of reality to a greater or lesser degree, depending on the intensity. Information in favor of the exposure is frequently perceived in exaggerated form, while changes in the market that might prove harmful are hardly noticed. At best, unexpected events that threaten the trader's position cause him to clear it, or to realize the profit.

Exposures that turn out to be successful are no problem. But things are different when positions do not develop as they should, which happens much more frequently. These also start with hope, and with the belief that the decision made was the right one. Initially, the trader will not respond to a small loss. Any slight doubts are soon removed by consulting a colleague, who does not want to contradict him out of consideration for his feelings.

Prices move slowly but surely in the wrong direction. Hope disappears and the first signs of anxiety appear, a "state of mind characterized by blocking determined and rational control of the personality" (Dorsch et al. 1994). The trader takes another detailed look at the fundamental situation in relation to the traded currency; the technical analysis did not show up anything untoward either. Discussions with friends are punctuated by repeated mutual confirmation of what they already knew anyway. Only the market appears to disagree, or at least it would seem so. The discussions increasingly turn into monologues, as the trader is not prepared to realize a loss just at the time when it appears to be at its worst. He postpones a decision to clear his position, for nobody is keen to lose face.

The anxiety phase proves fatal in particular for market participants who have entered an extremely large-volume position, following a previous run of success. Afflicted by greed or even euphoria, they are at a loss to understand what is going on. The conviction that they cannot go wrong completely clouds their perception of actual events in the market, even at this stage. Anxiety slowly creeps up on them and turns into a paralyzing fear.

The perception of the trader changes during the anxiety phase. He suppresses all unfavorable news and information, while simultaneously overvaluing the meaning of positive messages. Fear immediately turns into hope when the price finally starts to move in the opposite direction, which temporarily appears to reduce the threatened loss. This state of mind is experienced as encouraging, to such an extent that the trader is inclined to "reduce" the cost price through an additional purchase at the now lower price. He is no longer conscious of the fear to which he has become accustomed over time, as the human mind tends to ignore sustained stimuli. Some traders overcompensate, moving from a state of fear to the opposite state, recklessness.

Additional buying often turns out to be an unwise move, as the market frequently shows a small correction after a previous, perhaps somewhat exaggerated movement. Nevertheless, such positions have been known to turn out to be harmless, in that the price has actually again reached the now "improved" cost price for the trader, who is pleased to have escaped unscathed. The main thing is that loss of face has been avoided.

Additional buying is the same as entering into a new position, whose loss is not in the least reduced by this action. Any relief for the human psyche is only superficial: pressure and stress on the trader will increase once prices again move contrary to the exposure. Doubling the size of the position doubles the pressure, and the trader will find that fear rapidly turns into panic.

While an actor with a smaller position might already have dispersed with it during the anxiety phase, usually too late of course, a market participant with a large stake will at first hardly be able to respond. This is particularly the case with an actor who was previously successful and hence euphoric. He is paralyzed and cannot understand the market; he seems to have become speechless. Contact with friends and colleagues has more or less dried up, as they dare not speak to him. His eyes are locked on to the monitor listing the prices. The point at which there is no longer any hope has arrived.

Suddenly, the entire exposure will be liquidated in one go. The psychological pressure or pain of possible failure and the hopelessness of the situation are so intense, and have increased to such an extent, that they invoke an act of desperation.

The trader has to recover for the next few hours. Mistakes are analyzed carefully, guilty parties are sought and often found. The disaster is usually blamed on some information, or a rumor, or other people's erroneous opinions, which have led the trader astray. Next time he will be better informed and not listen to certain people. Next time he will start trading cautiously with a small position, but after he has regained his confidence, he will go on to do greater deeds. A new cycle is about to start.

Weighing up the various emotional stages that arise during the profit-and-loss cycles, we must conclude that any extreme circumstances, even if positive, can be dangerous. There will be a change in information processing immediately upon entering a position. The stronger emotions will produce a distorted view of new data and messages that is much less objective than before. The actor is blind to all messages and rumors that contradict his exposure, while positive information is perceived in an exaggerated form. This applies as early as during the phase characterized by hope. In the case of joy or anxiety, a stronger filter is applied to the information. Things are not so bad in the case of joy, as a retreat from the market in case of doubt will still provide a profit. The consolation of a profit, even though not always sufficient to cushion later losses, remains, even if one had initially hoped to do much better. The problem with anxiety, however, is that the actual duration of the anxiety phase is extended by intermittent periods of hope; these small shimmers of hope are frequently as intensive as the total anxiety experienced previously, and sometimes they are even more intense.

Information is of little use in a mood governed by greed or panic. On the one hand, people tell themselves that they will be proved right anyway; on the other hand they may be completely paralyzed through panic. Information has no role to play in the extreme states of euphoria and desperation.

We should emphasize again that this is a story only about emotions as they might be experienced by a market participant or in fact by any individual who earns a living through money. Many people will say, "I've always known that" or "That's all very well as far as emotions are concerned but they can't be measured, as each person is different."

People do differ, but there are many typical patterns of behavior observed again and again, which are found, at least potentially, in all market participants. Some market participants may panic, as a result of marked anxiety, sooner than other people whose nerves are stronger. But being equipped with stronger nerves does not prevent panic from setting in at some stage. Basically, everyone runs the risk of no longer being capable of making rational decisions under pressure. This applies just as much to the many other types of behavior that are described in this book. There will always be certain departures from rational behavior that affect everyone to a greater or lesser extent.

The systematic analysis of non-rational behavior begins in Chapter 3. The discussion and analysis of systematic departure from rational behavior requires that we understand clearly what rational behavior is. How is rationality displayed? How do we define reason? We will discuss this in the next section when we describe the actions of a calculating and thoroughly rational market participant.

MAXIMIZATION OF EXPECTED UTILITY: MENTAL ARITHMETIC WITH EARNEST COLDHEART

In economics, the concept of *Homo oeconomicus* is used as an ideal example of a person who is thoroughly rational (reasonable) in their thinking and acting; let's call this person Earnest Coldheart. Many theories are based on this ideal, although some practical recommendations, for instance in relation to optimum portfolios, also assume the same degree of rationality as exercised by Earnest Coldheart, not only in individual market participants but in all of them (Markowitz 1952, Markowitz 1959, Sharpe 1970).

But what exactly is Earnest Coldheart's rationality based on? It is difficult to give a clear-cut answer to this question, not least because a glance at the literature in question soon indicates that you could write an entire book on this subject (e.g. Kirchgässner 1991, Rescher 1993). Rationality always goes together with a certain evaluation principle in an economic context, used here to study Earnest Coldheart, namely maximization of expected utility. This principle is explained iniitally in general terms as follows.

Rationality means maximization of expected utility

Earnest Coldheart is always trying to improve his economic situation. Time after time he chooses the alternative that yields the greatest benefit. Nearly all decision-making situations, however, contain uncertainties. This naturally applies to financial markets in particular, as such uncertainties are traded there. The issue as to who will run which risk, and therefore have a chance of a commensurate profit, is ultimately a question of who buys which securities. One of the consequences of the inevitable uncertainty is that Mr Coldheart generally cannot estimate the exact benefit resulting from a decision. He therefore needs to consider probability and incorporate it into his calculations in order to arrive at a rational decision.

How do you go about accounting rationally for probability? The calculation of expected value presents a generally recognized principle of taking into account probability. The expected value for an alternative is found when all possible consequences of this choice are multiplied by their probability and subsequently summed. It would then be rational to choose the alternative with the highest expected value. This process can be explained with the aid of an example.

Say Earnest Coldheart faces a choice between two alternatives. The first one consists of tossing a coin: he will receive $500 if heads are uppermost, but he will have to pay $200 if tails are shown. The second alternative is a bet, in which he will receive $200 if his football club wins next Sunday, but he will lose $100 if they draw or lose. He estimates the probability for each alternative in order to make a rational decision.

This is easy in the coin-tossing game, where the probability that he will win equals 50 per cent. Less obvious, however, is the probability that his football club will win. As he has complete confidence in the team, and the opponents have not exactly distinguished themselves in the past, he considers the matter and arrives at a probability of 80 per cent in favor of a win. He now calculates the expected value as follows:

Tossing coins: $(50\% \times \$500) + (50\% \times -\$200) = \$150$
Football bet: $(80\% \times \$200) + (20\% \times -\$100) = \$140$

The gamble with the coins has a higher expected value than the bet in favor of a win by his football team, and is therefore chosen as a rational decision.

This example shows the basic principle of maximization of expected value. It does not show the principle of expected utility. There is a small but vital distinction between these two principles, which is explained below with the aid of the St Petersburg game (Bernoulli 1738).

The St Petersburg game involves tossing a coin. A participant wins \$2 if the coin comes up tails, whereupon the game ends. The coin is tossed again if heads is uppermost. The participant receives double the first amount if tails comes up again, i.e. \$4, and the game ends. Should heads come up, then the coin is tossed a third time. The win is again doubled on tails, i.e. it now amounts to \$8. In the case of heads, the game is continued as above, with further doubling. The game ends when tails comes up. The participant always wins; only the amount of the win is uncertain. The probability of a gain of \$2 is 50 per cent, of \$4 it is 25 per cent, and of \$8 it is 12.5 per cent. The expected value in respect of this game is therefore:

$$(\tfrac{1}{2} \times \$2) + (\tfrac{1}{4} \times \$4) + (\tfrac{1}{8} \times \$8) + (\tfrac{1}{16} \times \$16) + \ldots =$$
$$1 + 1 + 1 + 1 + \ldots = \text{infinity}$$

Logically speaking, the rational Earnest Coldheart should prefer the St Petersburg game to any certain gift of money, however large, on the basis of the infinitely high value. Theoretically, he would reject an offer of \$1 million or even \$1 billion in order to participate in this game. Nobody would call this a reasonable decision, however cold their heart or cool their head.

This implausible overvaluation of the St Petersburg game resulting from the calculation of expected value disregards the fact that the usefulness of additional money decreases as more is received. People would certainly be pleased with the excess if they won \$200 instead of \$100. But would it represent such a large difference if one received \$100 million plus \$100 instead of \$100 million? The utility of the additional \$100 is therefore much less in the second example than in the first. This is precisely why it is more sensible to focus on utility, rather than on the amount of money, when calculating expected value. In the case of Earnest Coldheart, this means that he chooses the alternative that brings him the highest expected utility. This is the principle of maximization of expected utility.

A further aspect of evaluation in the St Petersburg game, and therefore also in the evaluation of all uncertain alternatives when faced with a decision, lies in a person's attitude to risk. Many people attempt to avoid all risks. Others enjoy some degree of uncertainty. It offers some excitement in their otherwise slightly dull everyday lives. The enjoyment of risk is so strong that many people will pay to go to a casino to gamble, even though statistically they are always the losers.

Risk aversion is seen as a rational characteristic in the literature of economics. The view that it is rational to value risk negatively to a certain extent is not altogether without problems. We will return to this in greater detail in Chapter 5, when we have a clearer understanding of some facts not yet discussed.

In summary, Earnest Coldheart maximizes the expected value of his personal utility at each decision. Also, the utility of money decreases as the sums increase. In addition, we may have to take into account a particular attitude to risk on the part of Earnest Coldheart. Who could take account of all this when calculating which decision to go for?

Easy: Earnest Coldheart calculates a "utility function", which assigns a specific "utility value" to each sum of money, which in turn lies somewhere along an abstract normalized scale between 0 and 1.

An example of such a utility function (*u*) for changes in capital between −$200 and +$500 is shown in Figure 2-1.

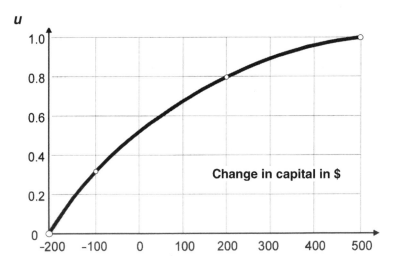

Figure 2-1   Example of a utility function.

The projection of the given values shows the following expected utility values for the two alternatives mentioned:

Tossing coins: $(50\% \times u\,\$500) + (50\% \times u\,(-\$200)) =$
$\qquad\qquad (50\% \times 1) + (50\% \times 0) = 0.5$

Football bet: $(80\% \times u\,\$200) + (20\% \times u\,(-\$100)) =$
$\qquad\qquad (80\% \times 0.8) + (20\% \times 0.3) = 0.7$

It is clear that the football team bet is suddenly valued higher when considering utility. The change in the ranking may be due to a reducing marginal utility and/or to the attitude to risk on the part of Earnest Coldheart. We are not interested in the reason, nor in the question as to how he arrives at this utility function. Presently it is sufficient to imagine that Earnest Coldheart is able to specify such a function with which he can master problematic decision-making situations on the basis of rationality.

What else does rationality mean?

Earnest Coldheart calculates the probability and expected utility for each alternative and chooses the one with the highest expected utility value. There are three more conditions for absolute rationality as portrayed by *Homo oeconomicus*: being fully informed with unbiased information, the absence of any distortions of judgment based on emotions, and the stability of the utility function.

Being fully informed with unbiased information
Earnest Coldheart shows unlimited interest in any information that is relevant to his decision, as he needs the information to be able to make a reliable calculation of the probability of financial success following his decision. A single factor that is not taken into account could reduce its usefulness later. He does not block out any information and he takes into account anything he needs to know, without distortion and in its entirety, unlike the currency trader in the previous section. He does not ignore news that does not suit him. Earnest Coldheart recognizes that this information is just as important as favorable news. He acts as accurately,

carefully and logically as a powerful computer when evaluating information.

Absence of any distortions of judgment based on emotions

Mr Coldheart is not so-called for nothing. He makes his evaluations and decisions in the same cool and careful manner with which he acquires and processes information. He knows that people's actions are all too often based on motives that can only be explained as psychological, and that stand in the way of economic action. His achievement is to no longer be driven by motives such as joy, greed, fear, panic, a desire to control or self-affirmation. Earnest Coldheart has no feelings.

Stability of the utility function

We must dig a little deeper to explain the third condition for rationality. We stated earlier that Earnest Coldheart bases all his decisions on his utility function, and calculates the expected utility value for all alternatives based on changes in capital relative to his actual wealth. But his wealth changes regularly after each decision. His wealth will increase frequently as he collects his information carefully, making sure it is comprehensive, and subsequently makes rational decisions in each case. Yet even Earnest Coldheart can be out of luck sometimes. Rationality does not pay off in each and every case.

To summarize again, the concept of the utility function always relates to changes in current capital. Is it possible to base the calculation of expected utility values on the same utility function, irrespective of one's current state of wealth? No: the evaluation of the utility of changes in capital changes with the state of one's wealth. We have also seen that utility relating to a specific increase in capital is greater in the case of presently low wealth than in the case of very great wealth. And the attitude to risk on the part of any individual could depend on the amount of their wealth. Earnest Coldheart must incorporate this in the process when he chooses an appropriate utility function for his current state of wealth.

He proceeds as follows. First he calculates his utility function over a period that is large enough for all theoretically possible

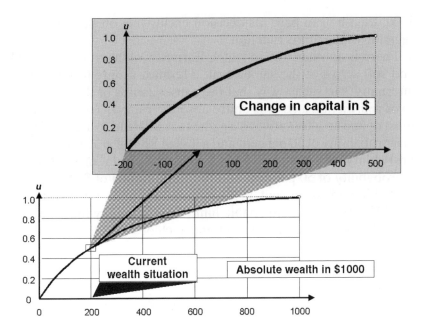

Figure 2-2 Derivation of a utility function related to a particular situation.

future capital positions to be included, as soon as he is faced with his first economic decision. He will start by imagining all possible situations accompanied by great or minimal wealth, in order to state clear-cut preferences that are valid for the period in question. His preferences are stable over time, and he does not change the evaluation of the subsequent absolute wealth should he manage to amass a large amount of capital or become impoverished in the meantime.

Once he has determined his utility function, he can always take the segment of the utility function in the vicinity of his then capital and use it to analyze the decision-making situation at any time and for any decision. Figure 2-2 depicts this situation.

Figure 2.2 shows the utility function in relation to the absolute wealth of Mr Coldheart. Assuming that his current wealth is $200,000 and that he faces a decision in a situation as described above, i.e. he must evaluate sums of money between $-200 and

$500, then he can base his decision exclusively on the respective segment of the utility function.[1]

There is another way in which Earnest Coldheart can proceed and still arrive at the same result. He must simply formulate all alternatives in such a way that the consequences of these alternatives represent exactly his entire absolute capital. To this end, he must define an alternative to a game that will lead to a gain of $500 at a probability of 50 per cent and a loss of $200 also at a 50 per cent probability. The alternative leads to a total capital of $200,500 at a probability of 50 per cent and to a total capital of $199,800 at a probability of 50 per cent, in the case of current capital amounting to $200,000. This would enable him to use his utility function that extends over the entire period and includes all possible capital points.

Earnest Coldheart's exposure

We have pretty much covered everything there is to say about the way Earnest Coldheart deals with exposure. He collects information before and during the exposure, of whatever nature. He works as carefully as a computer. He constantly calculates expected utility values for any alternative choices available at any particular time. Earnest Coldheart will probably use a computer on which a utility function program has been installed for this work. Mr Coldheart immediately acts on a calculation by the computer that a specific alternative offers the highest expected utility value. As soon as this is done, the computer analyzes new alternatives, using information extracted in the meantime by Earnest Coldheart. This process continues throughout the day. Earnest Coldheart shows no joy or anxiety, regardless of whether he wins or loses.

Earnest Coldheart's activities would appear very dull and uniform to an observer. But he will arrive at a higher profit than our currency trader in the previous section, who did not act

---

[1] The small segment, as well as the utility function relating to the absolute capital, has been normalized in utility values between 0 and 1, despite the much smaller period of time. This does not matter, as we only want to find out whether there is an alternative with a higher (expected) utility. This again shows that the values of a utility function cannot be based on their absolute size. In utility scales we use completely abstract scales, which may be transformed in a positively linear manner as required without changing their interpretation.

rationally all the time. Nevertheless, he is also subject to incidental influences. His profit is not certain, but tainted with risk, similar to the results achieved by the currency trader. Although Earnest Coldheart will not achieve more profit in every single situation, he will on average produce higher yields than the currency trader.

We need not state here that people made of flesh and blood cannot behave like Earnest Coldheart. The limited capacity with which people are able to process the stream of information bearing down on them leads them to simplify the thinking process and the preparations for their decisions. We know, for instance, that the human brain can master only seven pieces of information at any one time (Miller 1956). So how could one possibly absorb all relevant information and process it correctly? People are not computers; in fact they could be regarded as "cognitive misers"[2] (Fiske and Taylor 1991) who must carefully tend their capacity to process information. People use simplifying heuristics in order to control the complexity of information supplied by the environment. A heuristic is a mechanism for processing information that arrives at a quick result following little effort (e.g. Strack 1998, Anderson 1996). It will be clear that this method does not always guarantee an optimal result. We will introduce a number of these heuristics in Chapter 3, including their inherent problems.

Chapter 4 explores why people do not use stable utility functions in their calculations. Such behavior would mean that they evaluate their situations absolutely and that intermediate developments would be irrelevant to them. But people always evaluate relatively, never absolutely. They will be pleased about future wealth when they previously possessed less, but they will be annoyed if they previously had more. Chapter 4 shows the problems arising from such relative observation and evaluation.

As already mentioned, there is a whole series of purely psychological motives that clash with rational decision. Unless thay are depressed, people carry positive images of themselves, which they like to see confirmed in many forms. They have a basic need, for instance, to control a situation and to make right decisions at all times. Denied this, which can happen easily, these as yet unfulfilled needs determine their further actions. People often revert to panic

---

[2] Congnitions represent opinions, beliefs, units of knowledge or more general processes of awareness (Frey and Gaska 1998).

actions, which defy common sense, when losing control of the situation. In the case of a wrong decision, most people seek to justify it anyway, even if they incur high costs in doing so. It is easy to see that this soon results in irrational patterns of behavior, as shown in Chapter 5.

Chapter 3

Dams to combat the flood of information

Strategies for controlling difficult situations

With few exceptions, nobody can fully master real decision-making situations, regardless of time and effort, due to their complexity. There are usually a great number of factors involved; moreover, they may influence each other, which renders it almost impossible to look at them in isolation. Uncertainty always remains in respect of the actual degree of influence, their dependency on other factors and their effect. How can market participants handle the perpetual flow of information descending on them? How can they draw the right conclusions and judgments from all these updated messages and events needed for profitable trading, considering also that hardly any decision situation is stable over time? What applies today may be out of date tomorrow. This applies to currency and stock markets in particular, where frequently only seconds are available for a response. Market participants resolve this by trying to simplify the content of the messages and their possible influence on trading as much as possible.

People must use resources at their disposal for a decision-making process as efficiently as possible. We mentioned the "cognitive miser" in the previous chapter, who regularly uses heuristics in order to control extreme complexity. Heuristics are rules or strategies for information processing, which help to find a quick, but not necessarily optimal, solution. Heuristics are used when people are overwhelmed by information or have no time to process information thoroughly: remember that people can assimilate at best no more than seven units of information simultaneously. Heuristics are also often used when a problem does not seem very important or when people have no prior experience of resolving a particular problem (Aronson 1994). All this applies to short-term oriented traders in the financial markets who, more than any other market participants, are under enormous time pressure as well as pressure to perform. They cannot usually process the large quantities of information available to them.

Heuristics can be used consciously or subconsciously. A typical case of conscious heuristics can be found in a currency trader who needs to respond quickly to new information. The US labor market statistics are, for instance, always announced in two parts by the news agencies: the unemployment rate and the non-farm payroll, which indicates the number of newly created jobs in the non-agricultural sector. As the non-farm payroll is generally regarded as the more important of these, traders will consider only this for their possible exposures when an announcement is made. The unemployment rate will be ignored as part of a conscious heuristic strategy, due to time pressure, as one would likely "miss the bus" by the time a careful analysis of both figures was carried out.

The decision maker usually knows that conscious heuristics carry an inherent risk, and may lead to results that might not be 100 per cent reliable. A currency trader, for instance, may encounter a dilemma in that the non-farm payroll contains signals different to the unemployment rate. In contrast, the results of subconscious heuristics are, of course, far less transparent and carry risks arising from accidentally distorted perception and assimilation of information.

The following explanation is therefore based on subconscious (risky) heuristics.[1]

---

[1] The main research findings can be found in Kahneman et al. 1982; Strack 1998 also offers a good overview.

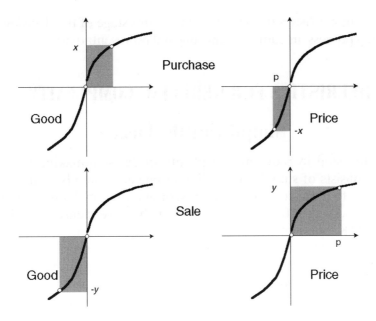

Figure 3-1   Overview of heuristics.

There is no clear-cut distinction between conscious and sub-conscious heuristics. The authors, for instance, have experienced that initially subconscious processes grow increasingly trans-parent with increased involvement with this subject, until they can be observed almost consciously. The same learning outcome is intended for readers of this book. Only those who recognize the heuristics to which they are susceptible will be able to neutralize to some extent the associated distortions in the perception and assimilation of information, and will therefore be able to make more rational decisions in the future.

People must restrict themselves to observing only the essentials when faced with high complexity in respect of a decision, i.e. they must reduce the many-layered aspects of a problem. This is dealt with later, where simplification heuristics, mental accounting and availability are discussed. Once the complexity of the decision-making problem has been reduced so that the "cognitive miser" is able to grasp it, the information must be processed and a judg-ment formed as soon as possible in order to arrive at a decision.

Judgment heuristics become relevant at this stage of the decision-making process, including anchoring and representativity.

HEURISTICS FOR REDUCING COMPLEXITY
Simplifying the facts

The first step in reducing complexity in decision-making situations consists of simplification. For instance, by simply rounding amounts to more convenient figures, or ignoring small differences when assessing information, providing they are clearly not significant (Kahneman and Tversky 1979).

An example will make this clear. A gambler can choose between a certain win of $50 or the chance to win $101 with a probability of 49 per cent. How does he decide? He focuses on essentials and simplifies the situation somewhat: the certain amount is easily grasped and processed cognitively as it is a round sum. The possible win, however, is still too complicated. Basically, the situation is that he can win $100 with a probability of approximately 50 per cent. The gambler will undertake this slight modification and then compare the alternatives with each other.

The simplification seems rational and unproblematic in this case. Yet such a plausible simplification can also produce unsound decisions, as the following example shows.

The manager of a German stock exchange department needs a young and ambitious trader to complement his team. Three applicants are short-listed, and they all give good impressions at their interviews. He decides to base his decision on the average school-leaving grade and the professional experience of the applicants. The applicants' profiles are as follows:

Applicant	School-leaving grade	Occupational experience
A	1.0	1 year
B	1.5	3 years
C	2.0	5 years

Imagine that the manager weighs up the candidates as follows: he prefers applicant B to applicant A in a straight comparison because B clearly has more experience and the grades are very close. Similarly, he chooses applicant C on the basis of a straight comparison between B and C. The small difference in the grade is in fact ignored in these two comparisons for reasons of simplicity. But when he compares applicants A and C, he finds that the grades are so far apart that he prefers applicant A, despite his comparative lack of professional experience. To summarize, A is worse than B, B is worse than C, and C is worse than A. The question as to whom should be appointed remains unresolved.

It also becomes clear that although it helps to simplify decision-making situations and facilitate cognitive control, ignoring small differences also adds the risk of arriving at non-rational conclusions if one is not careful.

Mental accounting

There are, of course, other ways of simplifying complexity. For instance, by ignoring possible relationships between potential commitments and projects. "Project" is used in the sense of any occupational or private commitment, such as purchase of share x, purchase of share y, or investment in a particular property, but also attendance at a concert etc. This context has generated the concept of "mental account" (Tversky and Kahneman 1981), according to which people keep not only a mental tab on the totality of all projects and their consequences but also a separate mental account in respect of each of their plans. People focus on one account in particular when weighing things up; relationships with other commitments or accounts are usually ignored.

This form of reducing complexity is certainly effective, if not entirely without problems. The general process of mental accounting is explained below with the aid of an example:

Situation A: You have purchased a ticket for a concert at a price of $150. Arriving at the concert hall, you discover that you have lost your ticket. The ticket office still sells tickets in the same price range. Would you buy another ticket?

Situation B: You have reserved a ticket for $150 to be collected. Upon arrival, you discover that you have lost $150 from your purse. Would you pay for the ticket, assuming you still have sufficient cash?

The two cases are identical from an economical point of view. In both cases, you find upon arrival at the concert hall that you have lost $150, and in each case you face a decision as to whether you will pay again in order to attend the concert, or whether to return home. Empirical research (Tversky and Kahneman 1981) has found that the majority of those questioned decided not to attend the concert in the first case, but would pay for the reserved tickets in the second case.

This inconsistency in behavior is easy to explain. The decision makers in both cases keep mental accounts, i.e. a "concert account" and a "general cash account". Attending a concert offers a positive value in the form of fun, entertainment and enjoyment of art, which is credited to the concert account (during the concert). This value is set off against the price of the ticket. The price has already been debited to the concert account upon arrival at the concert hall in the first situation. The purchase of a second ticket would increase the debit side of the account, so that the concert visit would suddenly cost $300. This might well seem too much for a concert, hence the reluctance to purchase a ticket amongst those questioned.

In contrast, the loss of $150 in the second situation will be debited to the cash account. This reduction in the balance, though annoying, does not affect the imaginary balance of the concert account. So why not attend the concert in the second situation? The example shows that the decision-making behavior in an economically clear-cut situation is affected by the fact that two separate accounts are kept, without allowing for interrelationships.

Why is a reduction in complexity through mental accounting so problematic in the financial markets in particular? Imagine, for instance, that Company A produces bathing costumes, and Company B produces raincoats. Both companies are new, extremely efficient and innovating, so that purchasing shares in these companies would seem very profitable indeed. A financial gain, however, depends to a large extent on the weather in both cases. Company A will produce huge profits if the weather is fine, while Company B will make a loss, even though this is kept to a minimum thanks to its efficient management. The situation is reversed in the case of bad weather.

Should we, as part of our mental accounting, evaluate a contract to buy shares in Company A in isolation from the purchase of shares in Company B, then we might decide to use the money for other purposes, taking into account the inherent high risk in each purchase. Either investment is too risky when seen in isolation. However, if we take into account the mutual effect of the uncertainty factor, i.e. the weather, then a combination of both shares becomes a lucrative, and at the same time secure, investment. Ignoring the (risk) interrelationships can therefore result in risks being assessed wrongly and in opportunities for profit being missed.

Mental accounting, however, can lead to even more serious consequences for decision-making behavior, which will only apply in the context of other psychological aspects. Readers will therefore encounter this phenomenon more than once in this book.

Availability

Not all information is available to the same degree. Certain data relating to a company's business prospects are more easily accessible to some people close to the company (insiders) than to outsiders, who may be able to access this information only with great difficulty. Nor are business TV programs available equally to everyone. Some people do not have a television, or the broadcast may take place at a time when some viewers are engrossed in their weekly sports program.

This, like similar cases, shows that everybody encounters some information that is easily available, and some information that is not. It seems plausible that the easily accessible information is used proportionally more often, if only on the grounds of efficiency, and that no cost or effort is spared in the case of an especially important decision in order to access information that is not easily available.

The financial section of a good daily newspaper, for instance, may suffice for a private investor to weigh up the market situation, and he will not be prepared to subscribe to an expensive specialist publication, which would also cost time to read. The trading division in a bank will often limit itself to a single agency news service, rather than subscribing to the services of three agencies, for reasons of cost. However, in both cases there is always the risk of receiving important information late, or perhaps not at all. In each case, the risk of this happening must be weighed up.

These considerations regarding the use of information with differential accessibility take place mostly at a conscious level. Recollection, however, concerns information that is activated mostly subconsciously. Recollections are also more or less available. The term "cognitive availability" could be used to distinguish it from actual availability.

Again, the psychologists Kahneman and Tversky (1973) studied empirically how cognitive availability affects the judgment of probability and frequency. They showed that decision makers put a higher value on the probability frequency with which a particular event occurs, the more examples there are available for this event. They named this "strategy availability". We are dealing with a heuristic that reduces complexity by ignoring information (recollections that are not easily available, or not available at all), leading to direct consequences for judgment. Take an investor who has never experienced a crash on the stock exchange, and who therefore has no recollection of such an event. He will assess the risk of a crash at a lower level than someone who has already experienced a sudden drop in the price of shares.

If recollections play an essential role, then factors that affect their cognitive availability can also lead to distorted judgments. These include four factors that are independent of the actual frequency – recency, conspicuousness, vividness and affective congruence – in addition to the subjective frequency with which examples for a particular event are stored as memories.

Imagining the human memory as a depository, it becomes clear that recent events carried in the head are considerably easier to access than those that took place some time in the past (Wyer and Srull 1980). Anyone who has just listened to a news broadcast about an aeroplane crash is likely to overestimate the probability of aeroplane crashes. The probability is overestimated not only on the basis of recency, but also because the event is conspicuous. It has been shown (Lichtenstein et al. 1978) that the probability for highly visible causes of death (e.g. an aeroplane crash) is clearly overestimated and that the probability for less visible causes of death (e.g. heart attack) is considerably underestimated. Similar results were shown in a study of information processing in the stock markets (De Bondt and Thaler 1985). These results showed that people always responded emotionally, or even in an exaggerated fashion, to highly visible recent information, e.g. surprising news.

A further aspect that may result in distorted judgment is the vividness of certain events or information. Concrete, emotional or easily pictured information carries more weight than abstract data (Nisbett 1976). For example, an importer needs US dollars but is not yet sure about the right time for the transaction. He studies a stack of boring forecast papers, and he has also asked a technically oriented analyst whether he should trade immediately or wait. The forecasts, as well as the analyst, assume that the price of the dollar will continue to fall – the importer should therefore postpone his purchase of dollars. A friend calls the importer shortly after, and tells him in vivid language that he has incurred a bitter loss of some 100,000 euros by delaying a recent purchase of dollars. This horror story causes the importer to buy his dollars immediately. The unemotional opinion, on which two experts were agreed, was countered by a single, but vivid, message that led to a rejection of the original analysis.

Any memory of an actual experience that is stored is accompanied by the same initial mood. The sudden death of a relative is stored in association with a very sad mood, while the birth of a child is associated with a particularly joyful mood. Affective congruence refers to the fact that recollections associated with a particular mood will be easier to access when in a similar mood (Schwarz and Bohner 1990). The relevance for investors on the stock exchange lies in the fact that they tend towards a positive price prediction when in a good mood following some gain, and that they will see the current market situation in a pessimistic light if they are in a bad mood following a run of bad luck.

Ignoring information

Selective perception
In addition to availability, there are other psychological mechanisms that cause people to ignore information. It is not only due to

the brain's limited capacity for absorption that some of the information is ignored. Often people do not wish to perceive everything. People tend to ignore information not only consciously but also subconsciously, when it "does not suit them" or when they expect to receive completely different information.

Impressive proof of this effect (Bruner and Postman 1949–50) can be obtained when the five playing cards shown on the inside front cover are shown to research subjects for about two seconds, after which they are asked which cards they have seen.

The surprising thing is that hardly anyone notices the marked card on top, even though the black three of hearts is not a true playing card. The expectation to see cards with red hearts and diamonds or black spades and clubs is so strong that a minimum of visual information suffices to recognize a "normal" colour. Out of a total of 1000 listeners at various different venues, only one person recognized the playing card mistake immediately. Most people need more than five seconds to pick out the fake card. The vast majority saw the black three of hearts as "normal" or perceived it as a three of spades. In the first case, the playing card symbol was changed subconsciously to match a shape (heart), while in the second case the colour was changed to black. In a few cases (on average, one in 50 people), individuals believed to have seen a red three of hearts, i.e. they stated that of the five cards, three were red. Conclusion: an extremely deep-rooted expected observation led to a false perception.[2]

Something similar can happen when, for instance, a tense currency trader is glued to the telephone waiting for an announcement on the US balance of trade figures, or another important economic statistic. A particularly high deficit – there are rumours of $17 billion – is expected for the previous month and people are prepared for the worst. The colleague at the other end of the line passes on the figure "twelve point twenty" (i.e. 12.2 billion) to the extremely pessimistic trader a fraction of a second before the usual information services; the trader hears only the last part, "twenty", and shouts out "twenty" in the dealer room. The others take this

---

[2] Personal motives, social influences and the frequency of earlier observations determine the strength of the expected observation (Lilli and Frey 1998). We would recommend the literature on hypothesis theory in social observation to anyone interested in the phenomenon of expected observation.

figure as read and respond immediately. The trader then sees the figure "12.2" appear on the screen and pales visibly.

Even analysts who are not under such time pressure select only the data from the wealth of information available that fit their theoretical construction and their personal preformed concept of the world (Hunter and Coggin 1988), and that match their current forecasts. Thus different forecasts from analysts are based on their different personal observation spectra. A particular expectation can even lead to contrasting interpretations of the same facts (e.g. Frey and Stahlberg 1990 for the construction of expectations in stock markets). Should an analyst expect rising stock prices, then he will consider news of an increase in the unemployment figure as a sign of further price rises, as the risk of inflation is reduced. On the other hand, he would consider a higher unemployment figure as a signal for slower growth in the economy and therefore a further drop in prices, if he assumes falling stock prices.

Selective observation is particularly active when people assess their own decisions after the event. Everyone wants their decisions to be the right ones. They will therefore be subconsciously selective as far as information is concerned. So, if a person has chosen to buy a particular make and model of car, then they will look for information that advertises the benefits of the car ordered. The advantages of the other alternatives, which were considered prior to the decision, are belittled. As a result of this so-called "spreading apart effect" (Brehm 1956), the person will linger on advertisements for the car they ordered when leafing through a car magazine, rather than advertisements for alternatives that were rejected (Ehrlich et al. 1957). We will discuss this phenomenon in greater detail in Chapter 5.

Contrast effect

A stimulus that cannot be distinguished from its environment will not be perceived. At this stage, we consider the consequences in relation to the perception of information, although the effects will be discussed fully in the next chapter, together with "relative evaluation", as was the case earlier with selective perception. We know, for instance, that information that is presented against a contrasting background is often perceived disproportionately (Aronson 1994).

For instance, the effect of individual colour contrasts on viewers in the presentation of news has been compared in experiments (Zimbardo 1995). These showed that black text on a yellow background is absorbed considerably better than information printed in grey on a white background. This issue has come to the fore only recently in currency trading firms. Workstations are currently equipped with numerous screens, which show messages in different colours. It is well-known that this causes distortions in perception.

Contrast effects are deployed daily in advertising and sales. The attraction of an offer can be increased significantly if it is contrasted with a similar but worse (illusory) alternative (Farquhar and Pratkanis 1993, Pratkanis et al. 1989). Imagine that you have been looking, without success, for a new apartment to rent. It has now become urgent because your existing rental contract has been terminated, and a date has been set for the move. A real estate agent first shows you a run-down, shabby apartment that is desperately in need of renovation. On hearing the rent demanded, you reject the offer. The real estate agent suggests a quick visit to a second apartment, as he would not like to lose your custom. He leads you into an apartment of average appearance; the rent, however, is higher than for the first one. You are keen to sign up because you are fed up with looking. The agent is also pleased – he had been afraid that he would not be able to let the apartment at all.

The contrast effect also plays a role in the case of a market participant who is inundated with profit messages about a particular share, and who subsequently receives a forecast that is a little worse but still good. And how does a currency trader regard a small upturn in the price of the dollar after it has been falling continuously for two weeks? Both pieces of information, although basically unspectacular, are regarded in such a dramatic light only because they contrast sharply with the previous messages. They would have hardly been noticed without this contrast effect.

Effects based on the order of presentation:
primacy and priming effects
The order in which several pieces of information are presented is important. Availability tends to ensure that the last mentioned remains uppermost in the mind, as it is the most recent and will

therefore be considered most frequently. However, this effect is countered by the usually more effective primacy and priming effects.

A classic experiment (Asch 1946) is often cited to explain the primacy effect. A hypothetical person, Steve, was judged by two different groups of subjects. Steve was described by Group A as "intelligent, industrious, impulsive, critical, stubborn and jealous", and by Group B as "jealous, stubborn, critical, impulsive, industrious and intelligent". The same characteristics were mentioned, but in reverse order. The relevance of the primacy effect, which means that in general the first-mentioned characteristics have more influence on the perception and evaluation process than those mentioned later, can be seen from the fact that Group A clearly rated Steve higher than Group B.

The primacy effect can also be observed in market participants who are presented with the US labor market data in the form of short texts or headlines, rather than in figures, as above. Compare the following sentences:

> US unemployment rate at a historical low but growth of non-farm payroll jobs less than expected.

> Growth of non-farm payroll jobs less than expected but US unemployment rate at a historical low.

The majority of market participants are likely to judge the economic situation in the USA considerably more positively from the first statement than from the second. The first piece of information has more influence than the second.

There are two explanations for the primacy effect (Aronson 1994). Concentration decreases as more information is absorbed, i.e. later pieces of information are automatically accorded less attention so that they tend to be given less weight when all information is considered together. On the other hand, the first impression would generally seem to be given more weight.

The first piece of information also plays an important role in the priming effect, as it affects the interpretation of subsequent information: it acts as a catalyst for further pieces of information (Felser 1997). An example is a game popular amongst children where someone is asked to say the word "blood" a few times in succession. When asked which traffic light colour signifies that cars can proceed, many answer "red". The colour red was obviously associated with blood.

A description of an experiment will help to explain the priming effect (Higgins et al. 1977). A group of subjects had to remember several positive words describing characteristics, such as "adventurous", "self-assured", "independent" and "persistent". A control group were asked to do the same with negative characteristics, such as "carefree", "conceited", "solitary" and "stubborn".

Both groups then had to judge a hypothetical person, Donald, whose conduct was highlighted. Donald's enthusiasm for parachuting was classed as an expression of his adventurous spirit by the first group, while the second group regarded this dangerous hobby more as an example of his "carefree" attitude. The fact that Donald was well aware of his strong points was regarded as self-assuredness by the first group, and by the second group as conceit. The labels provided during the first step in each case determined to a considerable extent how subsequent information was interpreted. Priming effects are therefore ultimately another consequence of availability.

The priming effect is very relevant to advertising and news reports in the media. The behavior of readers, listeners or viewers, for instance, is clearly affected by a change in the contents and importance of news broadcasts (Iyengar and Kinder 1987). Similarly, the way information relating to the financial markets is reported, the order in which information in ad hoc announcements by companies is presented, and the way in which analysts are introduced can determine the response from the audience. Even the interpretation of subsequent messages can be influenced in this way. The different layout of labor market data is only one example amongst many.

QUICK JUDGMENTS

Having described the three heuristics for reducing complexity in the previous section (simplification, mental accounting and availability), as well as effects resulting from ignoring information, we now introduce the heuristics for quick judgments. Once the complexity of a situation has been reduced to a manageable level, there remains the need to resolve the decision problem as quickly as possible. This generally demands particular judgments, e.g. in the form of estimations, probability, predictions, classification or cause-and-effect relationships. Heuristics are used to arrive at a quick judgment; they can, however, also systematically distort judgment in certain circumstances (Strack 1998).

Anchoring

A capacity for quick judgment is also in demand in the financial markets, particularly for forecasting movements of interest rates, stocks or currency prices. Most people tend to base their estimations or assessment of information initially on a first source or reference value (anchor) and subsequently to increasingly adapt this to the real value, taking into account further information, or via a more detailed analysis (adjustment). There is nothing wrong with this, provided the adjustment process is completed. Empirical research, however, shows that this is often not the case; rather, the adjustment process is regularly cut short and is therefore incomplete, i.e. the original value (anchor) is afforded too much weight.

An experiment (Tversky and Kahneman 1974) may help to explain this. Subjects were asked to estimate the percentage representing African states in the United Nations. They were divided into several groups. Each group was assigned a random number between 0 and 100 with the aid of a wheel of fortune. The first group received a value of 10, the second group a value of 65. The subjects had to indicate whether their estimate was above or below the random figure. In the following stage, the participants in the experiment were asked the actual figure, and it was found that the random number produced by the wheel of fortune clearly influenced the result. The average estimated percentage of African states in the United Nations amounted to 25 per cent in the first group, whose randomly allocated figure was 10, while the average estimate in the second group, with a randomly chosen number of 65, was 45 per cent. It would seem that even a randomly chosen number acting as an anchor value had a strong effect on the estimates provided by the subjects.

In another example, students were divided into two groups. They had to estimate spontaneously the outcome of a sum within five seconds. The first group had to estimate the following multiplication:

$$1 \times 2 \times 3 \times 4 \times 5 \times 6 \times 7 \times 8 = x$$

and the second group had to estimate the result of the multiplication below:

$$8 \times 7 \times 6 \times 5 \times 4 \times 3 \times 2 \times 1 = x$$

The outcome was amazing: the first group estimated the answer to be 512 on average, while the second group's estimate was 2250. The actual answer is 40,320 (Kahneman and Tversky 1982a).

This example shows that the students most likely focused on the first few figures of the sum. They soon saw that this was a multiplication sum; they seem to have multiplied the first few factors, while estimating the remainder. This is the only explanation for the fact that the first group arrived at results that were relatively low. The second group – who probably also calculated only the first part of the task – arrived at a higher result due to the different presentation of the sum: reading from left to right, they would probably only have absorbed "8 × 7 × 6" under time pressure. Surprisingly, both groups underestimated the actual answer by a large amount, due to concentrating on the initial part of the sum.

Such a glaringly wrong decision points at an adjustment process that is insufficiently developed. Even the adjustment in the second group, which started with a high-value anchor, was not sufficient to arrive anywhere near the real answer.

Anchoring also affects the estimation of probability when judging events that are grouped together. The first effect arises with the estimation of probability that at least one of several improbable events will occur. Most people underestimate the risk of having an accident within a period of 50 years, having been told that the probability of being in a serious traffic accident within 12 months is 0.1 per cent (Eisenführ and Weber 1999). The actual percentage is $1 - 0.999^{50} = 5\%$. The probability of 0.1 per cent therefore establishes an anchor that is subsequently adjusted insufficiently to the proper value.

The reverse of this example will produce the opposite effect. If the probability to not have a serious traffic accident during the next 12 months is set at 99.9 per cent, most people will give a percentage that is too high when asked to estimate the probability of not encountering a serious traffic accident over the next 50 years. The probability for the latter event as the negation of the former quite logically is 100% − 0.1% = 99.90%. The probability in this situation amounts to 100% − 5% = 95%, analogous to the earlier calculation. Understandably, as the anchor is high (99.9 per cent) in the second case, it is not adjusted downwards sufficiently.

This preference reversal can also be explained with the aid of anchoring (e.g. Lichtenstein and Slovic 1971, Tversky et al. 1990). Consider the following two games presented to visitors at a Las Vegas casino:

Game A: Participants win $1700 with a probability of 30 per cent.

Game B: Participants win $450 with a probability of 97 per cent.

It was shown that most people would choose game B when offered a free choice. The researchers then asked the subjects which amount they were prepared to pay in each case for participation in the two games. Most subjects mentioned a higher amount (e.g. $450) for game A than for game B (e.g. $430). It became clear that this ratio was inconsistent: $430 equals game B, game B is better than game A, and game A equals $450. So $430 must be preferred to $450. It goes without saying that the latter is obviously untrue.

The so-called compatibility effect (Slovic et al. 1990) is responsible for this irrational reasoning. The different methods of questioning (focus on a scale that is compatible with the question) ensured that the attention of the subjects was diverted first to the amounts of money, and then to the probability of winning. This resulted in the subjects concentrating on the different amounts to be won when asked about amounts of money.

The anchor of $1700 resulted in a greater advantage for game A. As the adjustment process was inadequate (it was terminated by the low probability of 30 per cent in bet A), the preferred choice remained game A. In contrast, the subjects concentrated on the issue as to which game would bring a win sooner. The anchor of 97 per cent was thereby cancelled, leading to a preference for bet B, the reasoning being equal.

Anchoring plays a role in many forms in the financial markets as it is a phenomenon that is inherent in the process of estimation. An anchor need not necessarily be a numerical value, it can also be based on opinions or attitudes (e.g. those of friends or experts). External information, collected for instance from analysts, is also available as an anchor. Asking a "bull" about the Dow Jones, for instance, results in a comparatively high anchor value for the share index. This will still tend to be too high, even after (usually inadequate) adjustment on the basis of one's own estimates. Similarly, a lower value will result following consultation with a "bear".[3] It is also possible that the answers proffered by analysts (e.g. in their newsletters) are themselves influenced by cleverly placed anchor values. This may ultimately be reflected in the behavior of market participants (Maas and Weibler 1990a).

Even data and forecasts that initially appear to be unrealistic still have an anchoring effect. Imagine, for example, a situation in which the USA gross domestic product for the previous quarter was forecast to have risen by three per cent by the majority of economists. Then a completely different figure of 6.5 per cent is suddenly mentioned, which any market participant would say was completely unrealistic. It must therefore be wiped from memory. Nevertheless, most traders will not really be surprised if an actual figure of 5 per cent is subsequently announced. The 6.5 per cent is still fixed in their brains. This situation is similar to the one a jury finds itself in when the judge decides to delete something from the records, because it is not admissible as evidence. Some people, in fact, will remember it for this reason alone.

The current situation usually serves as an anchor if there is no information available from a third party on the magnitude of the estimate. The spot price will be looked up in order to use it as an anchor for estimating the price of the euro in two years' time, which is then adjusted downwards or upwards depending on economic knowledge and other information. If, on the other hand,

---

[3] Bulls are market participants who predict rising prices; a bear expects falling prices.

only a probability band is required for the future price of the euro, then people will usually consider how far the price could move upwards and downwards, and how probable the individual movements in question will be as part of the adjustment process. Overstrong anchoring to the status quo will often result in the forecast band being set too narrow, and an underestimation of the probability of extreme movements (e.g. Lichtenstein et al. 1982).

Representativity

A young couple would like to have six children. Which order of birth (G = girl, B = boy) is more likely: GGGGGG or GBBGGB? Most people consider the first series to be less probable than the second (Kahneman and Tversky 1972). But they are wrong. Both series are just as probable as each other, providing the sex of a child is not affected by that of the previous child. Unless this is so, we are dealing with independent events in both cases, and the probability for both series is identical, i.e. $0.5^6 = 1.5625$ per cent.

The cause of this false judgment is the different representativity of the two series. In general, representativity expresses a particular relationship on the part of an object (persons, objects, events) with an object class (e.g. groups). An object is representative of the object class if there is a high similarity with typical, or a large number of, representatives of this class (Strack 1998). We can easily see this in the example of the order of births. Several orders of birth ultimately give the same number of girls and boys: GBBGGB, GGBGBB, GGBBGB, BBGGBG etc., and we need to look very carefully to see the differences. Any small changes in the GGGGGG order of birth, on the other hand, are spotted easily, as the exceptional regularity will have been lost.

Representativity can be explained even more simply with the concept of schemata or thinking patterns. Representativity is high when an observation fits the pattern. It is low when no suitable pattern can be discerned or activated. A fitting schema in the case of the order of births would be: "The sex of children is random; that is why boys and girls are normally present in families with more than one child." All people carry numerous schemata around with them, acquired through past observations, personal experience or learning. These schemata may therefore be subject to distortions.

Representativity as a distortion of judgment appears in three forms. The first variant is the tendency to overestimate the probability of representative events. The second and third variants relate to the tendency in many people to overestimate empirical and causal relationships, or even to perceive these where none exist.

Overestimating probability

Overestimation of the probability of representative events was shown in the initial example when the representative order of birth was assigned a higher probability than the non-representative order. Neglect of the actual or objectively correct basic probabilities in accordance with the axioms of probability calculation is also a factor in the three fallacies described below, which are outcomes of estimated probability.

Weighing up related and unrelated events (conjunction fallacy): We know from probability calculation methods that the joint probability of two events occurring can never be greater than the probability of each individual event occurring. The event "friend arrives in the rain" cannot have a probability higher than 40 per cent if the probability that it rains tomorrow is 40 per cent and the announced visit by the friend has a probability of 80 per cent. It is surprising that many people frequently overlook this fundamental situation. It occurs when the joint event has a higher representativity than the individual events, as seen in the following example, also known as a "conjunction fallacy". As part of the experiment, a hypothetical woman, Linda, was presented to the subjects (Tversky and Kahneman 1983):

> Linda is 31 years old, very intelligent, and does not mince her words. She studied philosophy at university. As a student, she was closely involved with social justice and discrimination issues, and she participated in anti-nuclear demonstrations.

The subjects had to estimate the probability for the following statements relating to Linda:

1. Linda is a bank clerk.
2. Linda is a bank clerk and active in the women's movement.

The majority of the subjects (approximately 90 per cent) thought the second statement to be the most likely one. In accordance with representativity, we must assume that they very quickly remembered a schema of the type, "Whoever studies philosophy and is involved in social issues and discrimination may well also be active in the women's movement," so that the second statement about Linda would seem to them more plausible (or more representative) than the first statement.

This example can be applied easily to the currency market. As a similar study (Kiell and Stephan 1997) has shown, experts are not immune from wrong estimations of probability, which can easily creep into so-called scenario thinking. How probable do you rate the following scenarios (results in brackets)?

1. The US economy shows the first signs of overheating (41 per cent).
2. The rate of inflation in the USA is on the increase (44 per cent).
3. The Central Bank does its best to hold down the interest rate (26.9 per cent).
4. The US economy shows the first signs of overheating, subsequently the rate of inflation increases, and the Central Bank does its best to hold down the interest rate (35 per cent).

This small test shows that scenario 4, comprising the alternatives 1, 2 and 3, is deemed to be more probable than the individual situation 3.

Gambler's fallacy: A further typical false estimation is exposed by the famous example at the roulette table in the casino, called "gambler's fallacy". Assuming there is no cheating, probability theory indicates clearly that there is an equal chance of the colour black or red coming up in the next game (or in any subsequent game). Nevertheless, it is only human to assume that it is black's turn after a series of nine red numbers in a row, as people believe that chance evens things out. People think, "If red comes up again, then black would have not come up ten times in a row, which is extremely unlikely." Representativity has the same effect here as in the example of the order of birth. Yet it is not representative of a random process that the same event occurs repeatedly and consecutively (Tversky and Kahneman 1974).

Moreover, the odds that a black number will come up is just 50 per cent (if we include zero), and if the game is continued long enough, then black numbers are even more likely, so as to make up for the nine red ones – or so the argument goes. In reality, however, each individual game is independent of earlier games: the game would have to be continued infinitely for "compensating fairness" to take place, but zeros and the purses of the players would put an early stop to this. When zero comes up, all chips staked on red or black go to the house bank or casino.

Investors in the financial markets may also fall victim to the gambler's fallacy if they act on the saying, "What comes down must go up." Participants in an experiment (Maital 1986) could buy pretend shares whose prices moved completely at random. It was found that the majority of subjects expected rising prices after a long downwards trend and accordingly held on to them longer on average.

Confusing cause and effect (conditional probability fallacy): The third fallacy is based on the fact that usually condition and event are confused at least once when interpreting highly probable events that are conditional. The conditional probability fallacy is explained with the following example (Dawes 1988).

According to the newspapers, a US doctor amputated the breasts of 90 women in a high-risk group as a preventive measure, as 93 per cent of cancer of the breast occurs in members of this high-risk group. The doctor based his actions on the fact that the probability of cancer of the breast occurring was of the same high order for all members of this group. But further statements by doctors showing that 7.5 per cent of all American women have cancer of the breast, and that the high-risk group represented 57 per cent of all women, show that the surgeon had clearly based his action on a fallacy. If we indicate the event "patient has cancer of the breast" with "bc" and the event "patient is a member of the high-risk group" with "hr", then the probability for hr occurring under the condition that bc applies is 93 per cent. We are therefore dealing with a conditional probability. This is also expressed as p(hr | bc) = 0.93. The frequency of cancer of the breast amongst all American women is 7.5 per cent, so the a priori probability is therefore p(bc) = 0.075. The percentage of the high-risk group is

57 per cent of all women, therefore p(hr) = 0.57. The probability that the undesirable event of cancer of the breast occurs in a member of the high-risk group is therefore as follows, in accordance with Bayes' theorem:

$$p(bc \mid hr) = \frac{p(bc) \times p(hr \mid bc)}{p(hr)} = \frac{0.075 \times 0.93}{0.57} = 12.2\%$$

and hence is comparatively small.[4]

It seems that the schema "Whoever has cancer of the breast is typically in the high-risk group" was available to the surgeon in this example of representativity. Each patient in the high-risk group naturally fits into this pattern, which can therefore be activated quickly. It then forms the basis for assuming a high probability for breast cancer. The fact that condition and event are mixed up here is lost, just as was the case with the basic probability in respect of the gambler's and the conjunction fallacies.

Whether the perception of conditional probability leads to small or serious distortions of judgment depends on the actual distribution in the totality of perceptions. Another example will help explain this. There is a widespread view amongst the population that a typical currency trader is nervous and frantic. If we find ourselves in the currency-trading division of a large bank and we meet someone who seems nervous and frantic, then we will activate the schema in question in accordance with representativity and conclude that the person is probably a currency trader. In this case, the distortion of judgment is minimal as most of the people in a trading division will be traders, and therefore the probability of meeting a trader is quite high.

If, on the other hand, you encounter a person at 11.30 a.m. in a train station who seems nervous and frantic, then the a priori probability for the event, "This person is a trader", is very low, as nearly all traders are frantically busy in their office at this time. An estimated high probability that the person in the station is a currency trader, following the representativity heuristic, in this case leads to a serious distortion of judgment. This person very likely has a different occupation despite the representative trader characteristics.

---

[4] See, for example, Eisenführ and Weber 1999 on Bayes' theorem.

A final example of conditional probability concerns the estimation of the risk of a crash on the stock exchange. It is well known that most crashes take place October. In terms of probability theory, we say that the probability that a crash has occurred in October is relatively high, based on historical observation. Looking at the Dow Jones for the years 1929 to 1998, and defining a drop in prices as a crash when the share index loses ten per cent or more of its value over a period of a few days, then we find that a probability of 34 per cent applies, i.e. ten of the 29 crashes took place in October (expressed as p(October | crash) = 10:29 = 34%).

Share dealers often think, "It's October, so the risk of a crash is high." In this case, the conditional probability (p(crash | October)) is overestimated, as such drops in prices occurred during only ten of the 62 Octobers since 1929. This equals a probability of approximately 16.1 per cent. The condition and the event, or in a broader sense, cause and effect, have been confused.

Overestimating empirical relationships

The distortion caused by representation in this second variant is more serious than in the case of confusing condition and event, as the latter were actually individually present. Thinking in schemata often causes us to perceive relationships that are not there. Limiting ourselves to the perception of empirical relationships, we can also call this phenomenon "illusory correlation".

First an example. Many people assume a relatively high risk when estimating the risk of HIV in lesbians (Aronson 1994). In fact, not only is the HIV infection rate for lesbians lower than for male homosexuals, it is also lower than for all male and female heterosexuals. One of the reasons for this false estimate is representativity. It would appear that most people carry the following schemata in their heads: "Homosexuals are associated with a high risk of HIV" and "Lesbians are homosexuals". Both statements on their own are objectively correct, but the conclusion that lesbians have a high risk of infection is false. As people are careless when interpreting facts within a schema, as was shown for the perception of conditional probability, joining both schemata in this example and arriving at a false conclusion is easily done. People perceive an empirical relationship that does not exist, at least not to the extent stated.

Another apparent correlation concerns the stock exchange segment of the Neue Markt, which lists innovative high-tech companies whose shares are in great demand once they have gone public. These companies have, amongst other things, excellent prospects, which are anticipated by investors, and which accounts for their growing value.

A glance at the indicative profits on the entire exchange, however, shows us that this effect was generally transferred to other companies in the beginning, whose future prospects are less rosy, until fundamentally justified prices were restored after a period of time. There must have been many investors who imagined a relationship between going public and high growth rates in the case of high-tech companies. And the demand by these investors subsequently ensured that prices developed as they expected. The later fall, however, shows that this was an illusory correlation rather than an actual relationship (Ibbotson and Ritter 1995).

Overestimating causal relationships

The estimate of a future situation was based on observation in the past in the case of the risk of a crash (conditional probability fallacy) as well as in the example of the Neue Markt. Ultimately, this is the same as assuming a causal relationship. The following example shows how the perception of such a relationship can come about through representativity. Imagine two analysts who issue daily a short-term forecast on the development of the dollar price. Both analysts are observed for two days by a client. Analyst 1 issues two correct forecasts on both days, while analyst 2 gets it wrong on both days. The client will rely on analyst 1 rather than analyst 2 for the next forecast.

The correct or false forecasts are stored as schemata in the client's brain: "Analyst 1 offers correct forecasts and analyst 2 offers false forecasts." The client will therefore assign a higher probability of a hit for the next forecast to analyst 1, based on the first variant of representativity. In other words, the client assumes that the schemata created in the past will be continued in future. This, in turn, is nothing less than the assumption that analyst 1 is better than analyst 2. So an empirical relationship has been turned into a causal one.

An empirical relationship, however, does not necessarily mean a causal relationship, as shown in the stork example. Even though more children are born in countries with a high number of storks than in other countries, the high birth rate is not necessarily due to the storks (at least according to current science).

Assumed causal relationships must therefore be compared with the actual ones in order to estimate the extent of the distortion of judgment described. There is no doubt that analyst 1 might be better than analyst 2, as the quality of an analyst is based on his forecasts usually being right. In fact, analyst 2 could be the better analyst, but he was unlucky twice in a row. Two observations are insufficient for a conclusion.

On the other hand, it is true that in a sufficiently large group of analysts, there are a few who are always right, even over a fairly long period, based on laws governing the calculation of probability. Imagine a group of 4000 children who predict the movement of the dollar for the coming week by tossing a coin. The dollar will rise if heads is shown and will fall if tails comes up. One of the rules says that children who get it wrong are no longer allowed to play. In other words, half the children will be wrong in accordance with probability calculation, and they will drop out. One child still remains after a period of three months, having always got it right. Would the human resources manager in a currency trading division employ this child on the basis of his or her skills?

Empirical relationships do not necessarily signify causal relationships, but they do not exclude them either. People, on the other hand, are typically inclined to postulate on the basis of empirical relationships based on schemata when making predictions, assuming causal relationships. Actual causal relationships are generally overestimated, or a causal relationship is perceived where none exists.

A final example of an obviously overestimated causal relationship is the link between fashion and the financial world. It is said that share prices rise when skirt hems are higher. Surely it would be sensible to offer miniskirts for sale during a period of recession? Would this cause prices to recover?

Additional proof that causal links are overestimated
The inclination towards a premature perception of causal relationships, which is based on representativity, is supported by other

findings in psychological research. We know that people have a strong need to control their own situations, including their immediate surroundings (DeCharms 1968; see also Chapter 5). This need could be why people like to know the reasons for what is happening to them. People sometimes imagine something that is not real in order to satisfy this need for control, for example causal relationships (Stahlberg et al. 1998).

The so-called "attribution theory" (e.g. Herkner 1980, Meyer and Försterling 1998) relates to the question, to which causes do people attribute certain events? This theory focuses on events that relate to people's own actions or the actions of other people. It distinguishes two basic attributions.

We speak of dispositional attribution if the cause for an event is attributed to the actor or to his characteristics (disposition). A situative attribution relates to a cause that is attributed to a particular situation, for instance good or bad luck. One concept in attribution theory is the "fundamental attribution error", which means that people base the actions or results of other people on their skills and characteristics (dispositional attribution), rather than on situative influences (Ross 1977).

Usually, this is explained by the fact that generally situative influences are not available to the observer and that it is therefore easy for him or her to focus on more obvious factors. The client will probably not know under which external circumstances the analyses were compiled. Analyst 2 may have been under great time pressure, based his analysis on bad research, or fallen victim to selective perception. It is much easier for an outsider to imagine the characteristics that may have led to a better or worse forecast.

Chapter 4

Everything is relative –

even the evaluation of gains and losses

Every decision-making process can be divided into three stages: perception, assimilation and evaluation of information. The previous chapter described how people simplify complex situations and arrive quickly at a judgment. This discussion related to perception and assimilation. This chapter deals with the last stage, evaluation, in particular relative evaluation.

The theory of relative evaluation is based on fundamental findings in psychophysics. An example of acoustic perception will help explain this. A bird that suddenly starts to twitter can be heard clearly in a quiet wood. If the bird sings near a motorway, then it is likely that no one will hear it. In scientific terms, an acoustic stimulus at a certain volume will be perceived better if the background noise volume is lower. Weber's law summarizes it even more generally: the stronger the background stimulus, the stronger an additional stimulus must be for it to be perceived (Zimbardo 1995).

The basis of all perception is therefore not absolute magnitude, but differences between stimuli. As a result, the same observation may well have a different effect, depending on one's view or starting point. A classic experiment in physics uses three bowls: one filled with cold water, the second with lukewarm water, and the third with hot water. Subjects submerge their hands for a while in the cold water, and then put the same hand into the lukewarm water. Most people experience the lukewarm water as hot. People who first submerge their hands in the hot water then experience the lukewarm bowl as cold.

Relative perception is represented in psychophysics by adaptation levels, first researched in depth by Harry Helson (1964), who also named this phenomenon. The core idea of the theory states that judgments based on perception are influenced by previous experiences that people have encountered, i.e. the stimuli that the organism has registered. For instance, in an experiment a student estimated several weights between 200 grams and 500 grams, some of which were labelled "light", others "heavy", one as "medium", some "unknown" etc. A weight perceived as neutral would be more or less close to 350 grams, depending on the order and the way the experiment was set up. This would be the adaptation level.

In the case of the acoustic example, it means that the stimuli that are at the adaptation level are perceived neither as loud nor as quiet. Above the neutral point, they will be perceived as loud, and below it as quiet. The adaptation level differs from person to person. The adaptation level of construction workers used to the noise from pneumatic hammers, drills and pile-drivers will, for instance, be higher than average (Klix 1976), while a recluse would judge the snapping of a branch in quiet surroundings as being quite loud.

The phenomenon of relative perception can also be applied to the evaluation of facts; it therefore influences decisions and actions. Evaluations are particularly important for participants in the financial markets, as they often have to grasp and evaluate situations in seconds. The frequency with which this occurs is probably unique, although quick decisions are often required in other areas of life as well.

REFERENCE POINTS AND DECREASING SENSITIVITY IN EVALUATING OUTCOMES

People not only perceive their environment subjectively, they also evaluate it subjectively. The neutral point referred to at the beginning of this chapter is present in perception as well as in evaluation. We call this neutral point the reference point, an essential part of any decision when discussing judgments of outcomes of actions. Outcomes that are at the same level as the reference point are perceived as neutral, analogous to the adaptation level in psychophysics. Outcomes that are above the reference point are perceived as relative gains, whereas values below are seen as relative losses (Kahneman and Tversky 1979). The perception and evaluation of gains and losses is therefore dependent on the reference point. The decision-making behavior may change if the reference point is moved for one reason or another.

Most people choose the purchase price as a reference point when they have bought a share at, say, 125 euros.[1] It follows that people are pleased with a profit of five euros if the share rises to 130 euros. Should the share price drop to 120 euros, then a loss of five euros is the result. At first sight, this would seem self-evident; it has, however, far-reaching consequences when we consider that people evaluate events, outcomes and values with decreasing sensitivity, the further these are removed from the reference point (Christensen 1989). We will explain what this means in the next section.

A model for our evaluations: the value function

The following example will help explain decreasing sensitivity. Imagine you are going out to dinner. You choose roasted duck, which you consider a sumptuous dish, since you are very hungry; you are even willing to pay more than the $22.90 asked. You eat the duck, and the waiter asks if you would like another one. As you are no longer hungry, the benefit of the second duck will clearly be less than the first one, and that of a third (could you manage it)

---

[1] In theory, commission etc. should be added to the purchase price, but in practice these costs, which should not be underestimated, are frequently ignored.

would in turn be less than the second. Each additional duck therefore offers a decreasing additional value. Similarly, a first glass of beer on a hot summer's day can be a delight, while you would probably no longer be sure of the taste after the tenth glass.

Applying these examples to money, decreasing sensitivity as far as profits are concerned means that people are more pleased with the first euro gain than with the second one, but more with the second one than the third one etc. Decreasing sensitivity has the same effect in the loss zone, i.e. below the reference point: people are really annoyed about the first loss of euros, but less so with the second loss.

These findings were portrayed in the form of a value function, v, in prospect theory by the psychologists Kahneman and Tversky; an example is shown in Figure 4-1. The value function indicates the subjective value that a decision maker associated with a particular gain or loss.[2]

The reference point for the evaluation is situated in the center of the figure where the coordinates originate. The reference point corresponds to the cost price of 125 euros when applied to the earlier example of the purchase of a share. Evaluation is still neutral at this stage, hence value function, v, has a value of $v(125 \text{ euros}) = 0$. A positive evaluation is shown to the right of the reference point. The rectangle that has been drawn shows the decreasing sensitivity: the evaluation of an identical sum of money decreases as it is further removed from the reference point. One euro difference is still valued quite highly near the reference point, but the evaluation of each additional euro declines as it becomes further removed from the reference point. The decreasing sensitivity results in a curve to the right (concave) of the value function in the profit area. To the left of the reference point (the loss zone), we can see that the curve runs counter to the upper curve with decreasing sensitivity: the value function curves to the left (convex). The presentation of the value function must, of course, be regarded as merely conceptual. The degree of decreasing sensi-

---

[2] Prospect theory was developed by Kahneman and Tversky (1979). In its original form, it is concerned with behavior of decision makers who face a choice between two alternatives. The definition in the original text is: "Decision making under risk can be viewed as a choice between prospects or gambles." Decisions subject to risk are deemed to signify a choice between alternative actions, which are associated with particular probabilities (prospects) or gambles. The model was later elaborated and modified.

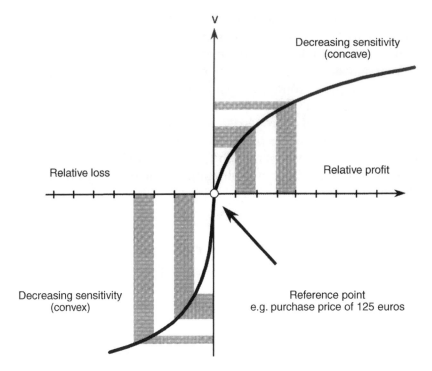

Figure 4-1   Value function in prospect theory.

tivity may not only vary from person to person but may also differ with each situation.

There are numerous everyday examples of decreasing sensitivity. For instance, many people will make a 30-minute detour in order to shop in the cheapest supermarket, rather the corner shop, saving a total of $300. And yet the same people are prepared to pay $1550 for a washing machine in a local shop, while the same model is for sale at $1520 in a shop 30 minutes' drive away. Considered from the point of view of the value function, this means that a sum of $300 is still close to the reference point, and the difference of $30 is perceived clearly. But when one is willing to spend $1550, then a difference of $30 is hardly noticeable as this is quite a distance from the reference point.

Decreasing sensitivity also plays a role in the phenomenon often seen in the stock market: an investor has recently acquired a share for 500 euros, and the price has fallen to 470 euros. He is probably quite annoyed about this loss. When the share subsequently falls from 260 to 230 euros in a further sharp drop in price, he will hardly feel it. He will think that it no longer matters.

You may have noticed that the curve in the loss zone is steeper than in the profit zone. This phenomenon is called loss aversion (Kahneman and Tversky 1979). It means that losses will be rated relatively higher than profits of a similar magnitude. Loss aversion, however, does not play a role in relative evaluation; we will explain the causes and consequences in Chapter 5. First, we will discuss some important effects of evaluation characteristics as portrayed through the value function.

How the attitude to risk can change: the reflection effect

Further typical behavior resulting from decreasing sensitivity is illustrated by the following example. A decision maker faces a choice: he can receive $1000 outright, or he can gamble, where he stands to gain $2000 with 50 per cent probability. Can we now predict his choice knowing what we do about decreasing sensitivity? He will normally choose the safe option of $1000, as shown in many empirical studies. Figure 4-2 offers an explanation.

Figure 4-2 shows that $2000 is not valued twice as much as a gain of $1000, due to decreasing sensitivity. The certain gain of $1000 is, on the whole, valued higher than the uncertain profit of $2000, taking into account the probability of 50 per cent.[3] We find that the decision maker has decided against the risky choice and favored the certain alternative, due to decreasing sensitivity: his behavior was risk-averse.

Repeating the experiment with losses instead of gains, we find to our surprise that the decision makers suddenly become risk takers, i.e. they decide against the certain loss and prefer to gamble, resulting in them having to pay either nothing or a higher sum. Using the same amounts as in the case of the profit example, we find that a loss of $2000 is not valued at twice the value of a loss of $1000 (based on decreasing sensitivity). Taking into account

---

[3]   Expressed as $v(\$1000) > 0.5\, v(\$0) + 0.5\, v(\$2000)$.

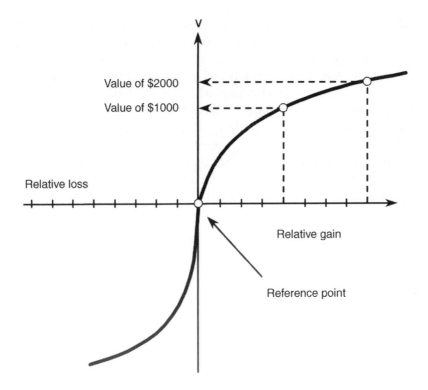

Figure 4-2   Explanation of the reflection effect.

the 50 per cent probability, a higher subjective value results for the uncertain loss than for the certain loss. The subjects choose the risky alternative.

We can conclude that decision makers behave in respect of risky alternatives in a way that is exactly opposite when moving from profit to loss. This is the "reflection effect" (Kahneman and Tversky 1979, Kahneman and Tversky 1982b).

The reflection effect leads to an interesting pattern of behavior when the reference point is manipulated through a particular presentation of the facts. In this context, we speak of a "framing effect". This occurs when different presentations of basically the same situation elicit different decisions. This effect is often used in advertising to influence the buying behavior of people. The correct location of the reference point and the presentation of decision-making problems play an important role in this respect.

A half-filled glass can be presented as either half full or half empty. The risk of an operation can, for example, be indicated by saying that one per cent of all patients die as a result, or one might say that the intervention restores the health of 99 per cent of all patients. A framing effect occurs when an operation is rejected in the first case and an operation is accepted in the second one.

The following decision-making situations will help clarify how framing can have an effect on economic decisions. These situations are often replicated in experiments. (The percentage of subjects who decided in favor of the alternative in question in a comparable experiment is shown in brackets [Kahneman and Tversky 1979, Kahneman and Tversky 1982b]).

> *Situation A:* In a game, you receive $1000. In addition, you have a choice between a certain gain of $500 (84%) or a 50 per cent chance of winning an additional $1000 and a 50 per cent chance of winning nothing (16%).

> *Situation B:* In a game, you receive $2000. In addition, you have a choice between a certain loss of $500 (31%) or a 50 per cent risk of losing $1000 and a 50 per cent chance of losing nothing (69%).

Looking at the total gains at the end of the games, we see that both game situations are identical, economically speaking.

Both cases center on the decision, whether one prefers a certain sum of $1500, or a gamble with which one can win $1000 with a probability of 50 per cent and the chance to win $2000 with the remaining 50 per cent. Most people, however, arrive at different decisions depending on the presentation of the facts.

This framing effect is easy to explain on the basis of the above considerations. We are dealing with a two-stage gamble in which the certain amounts in the first stage suggest a reference point for the second stage of the game. Amounts subject to risk must be evaluated in this second stage in which the subject has a different reference point in each case. The reference point for the second stage in situation A is $1000, and the additional sums are therefore relative gains. The reference point in situation B stands at $2000, so that the risk evaluation concerns relative losses. As the certain alternative in the profit zone and the risky alternative in the loss zone are preferred in accordance with the reflection effect, this reversal of preferred choices is logical. (Further examples of the

framing effect are described by Tversky and Kahneman 1981, and
Tversky and Kahneman 1986).

Why people like to let losses run: the disposition effect and the sunk cost effect

This section deals with the sunk cost effect, or rather the disposition effect shown as a special case of the sunk cost effect in two
stable behavior patterns of irrational action (see Chapter 5 for
more detail). We can show how the two effects can be explained
with the aid of the S-shaped value function or the reflection effect.

The disposition effect
The different evaluations of risk in the loss and profit zones lead
investors to realize paper profits too early in the case of short-term
transactions in the currency or stock markets, i.e. they decide in
favor of a certain profit and against the chance of possibly gaining
more or alternatively losing everything. If, on the other hand, they
have suffered a loss, they will decide to hang on to the stock and
rather than realize the loss. This is the same as a decision in favor
of a certain loss, as shown above, which is rated higher than the
chance to lose nothing, even if the latter includes the risk of an
increased loss. This inclination to realize profits too soon and to
hang on to losses for too long is also called the disposition effect
(Weber and Camerer 1998, Shefrin and Statman 1985, Gerke and
Bienert 1993). Figure 4-3 illustrates this effect by portraying the
purchase of shares after a rise in price and again after a drop in the
price.

   The investor has achieved a comparatively high increase in value
following a rise in the price, compared with the cost price. A
further rise in the price offers only a small increase in value in
accordance with the curve of the value function in the profit zone,
which bends to the right. He therefore does not hesitate to cash in
on his gain. The investor faces a drop in the value of his shares
in the loss area. A further drop in price does not matter as much
to him as the earlier price fall, in accordance with the flatter curve
of the function. Even if the loss was greater, then he will tell himself that this would not matter any longer. But he would be very

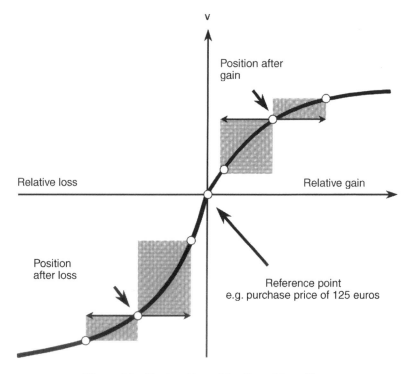

Figure 4-3   Explanation of the disposition effect.

pleased to see a rapid increase in value in the steep section of the function. He will tend to hang on to the loss even when there is no more than a minute chance that the price will recover.

We often hear the stock exchange rule, "Let profits run and stop losses." This rule is no doubt correct when price movements show a long-term trend. If we assume that further price rises are probable during the course of a current rally, or that a further drop in prices can be expected after a continuing downward trend, then it is best to get out immediately when dealing with a loss, and to hang on to the purchased share in the case of a profit.

The disposition effect, however, shows that investors judge their exposures on whether the value has risen or fallen after the purchase, for psychological reasons. As a result, losses are not realized and profits are stopped. The stock exchange rule therefore helps to counter the disposition effect. Many investors do not obey this rule, even though the explanation given is quite clear. The reason

may be that other psychological factors prevent market participants from realizing losses in good time. We will deal with these
later.

The sunk cost effect

This is the effect that costs already incurred in an exposure may
have on the willingness to invest further. It plays an important role
in our everyday behavior, as well as in the financial markets. Who
has not called a telephone help line and been told that they are in a
queue? You hang on for five or ten minutes, listening to the endless
muzak. All the time, you face the choice: will you hang up and
try again later, possibly only to be kept waiting again in another
queue? Or will you hang on a little longer? The automatic voice
promises that you are next in the queue. Hang up now? So near to
the goal. You give it another minute. It goes by without the desired
result – you hang up in desperation. The amount of precious time
invested and wasted in this way is countless.

Take another example. A student has an old car with a faulty
cylinder head seal, which the garage repairs for him. Cost: $1000.
The car goes well for a few days, until there is a problem with the
gearbox. The garage informs the student that repairs will cost
another $2000. They advise him not to have the gearbox repaired,
however, as the car is not worth the money: it would be lucky to
pass its next Motor Vehicle Inspection. It would be sensible to buy
a new car. The student, however, decides to have the car repaired;
he has, after all, recently invested $1000 in his jalopy. That is
wasted if he now decides to write off his car.

The similarity of this example with the disposition effect is clear.
The student made an investment that turned out unlucky for him,
just like the investor whose shares dropped in price. He also arrives
in a loss situation, as his car breaks down again after a short time.
He becomes a risk taker and is not inclined to put an end to this
commitment. The link with the disposition effect becomes even
clearer if we look at the sunk cost in both situations. Sunk cost
represents past costs "sunk" in a particular project, which cannot
be retrieved. The sunk cost in the case of the car is the irretrievable
cost of repairs amounting to $1000. The sunk cost represents the
fall in price since the purchase in the case of the disposition effect;
unfortunately, this cannot be recovered either. The disposition

effect therefore corresponds to the sunk cost effect in any other context. Many people tend to stick to projects in which they have already invested some money and which are situated in the loss zone, instead of terminating them (analogous to selling the shares at a loss or selling the car). We received the following email in response to a psychological survey of investors on the Internet (see Chapter 6 for further details). It shows what effect the sunk cost or the disposition effect can have on the performance of an investor.

The test result had me down to a t, my money keeps on decreasing, first in Emerging Markets, then writing options, now in the Neue Markt. All because I tried to recover initial losses. What shall I do now with my Neue Markt shares? My investment fund is undermined and devastated, the actual performance is just about minus 50%. Is my unfortunate situation hopeless? How can I make up the losses? My initial investment goal was to get a lot of money quickly. Now I know how to do it properly but first I have to get back to where I started. Can you offer me any advice?

Many an entrepreneur experiences the same thing. Take someone who has invested one million dollars in a project and concludes, after a period of 12 months, that it has not brought in the expected profit. Premature termination would therefore incur a loss. The entrepreneur employs an external consultant who, at a price, concludes that not everything has been lost: the situation is not hopeless if the entrepreneur is willing to invest a further $500,000 in the project. Most people would follow this advice, not in the hope of achieving a profit but merely in order not to lose face, i.e. to make up the initial loss. It might be more sensible to terminate the project and to invest time and money in a new, more profitable venture.

The sunk cost effect causes people to hang on for a disproportionately long time to unsuccessful projects, even if their failure can be predicted early on. This happens to an even greater extent if the success or otherwise of the venture is in the public eye (Beeler and Hunton 1997): the more people know about an unsuccessful project, the harder it is to abandon such an enterprise at an early stage. Something similar can be seen when, for example, the manager of a currency division has built up a strategic position that has strayed into the loss zone: his success or failure will be followed closely by many of his subordinates. It is therefore not surprising that people in responsible positions are particularly prone to fall victim to the sunk cost effect and its consequences. It is understandable from a human point of view that a manager prefers not to make mistakes in front of his staff. This has long-term fatal consequences for the success of his division, however. His behavior will be copied by some of his staff because the manager is supposed to set an example. Letting losses run could become a trading maxim.

The sunk cost effect can also bring about completely different, sometimes devastating, consequences. Take the Vietnam war, which was continued for such a long time partly because so much had already been "invested" in it and the sacrifices must not have been made for nothing.

The following example shows again that the tendency to not terminate projects that are subject to a loss can be explained by decreasing sensitivity alone. An entrepreneur simultaneously invests in three ventures: the first shows a loss of $1000, which represents a sunk cost. The second has so far shown no signs of either loss or profit. The third one has produced a gain of $1000 (see Figure 4-4[4]).

Which of the three projects would have precedence as far as working on them is concerned, given that a particular effort (e.g. working overtime for a period of 14 days) would bring an improvement of exactly $1500 in all three cases?

The decision would be based on the respective subjective additional value that can be achieved with the project. The smallest is the increase in value in the profitable project, as the additional $1500 is not regarded as a large result in accordance with decreasing sensitivity. The additional value is greater in the case of the neutral project, as a result of the effect of the originally still high sensitivity in the vicinity of the reference point in the profit zone. The increase in value is even higher in the case of the loss project, as the first increase in value in the loss zone will stand out in particular. This shows that decreasing sensitivity on its own increases the tendency to not terminate loss projects but to continue investing in them.

---

[4] Figure 4-4 omits the kink in the value function caused by loss aversion.

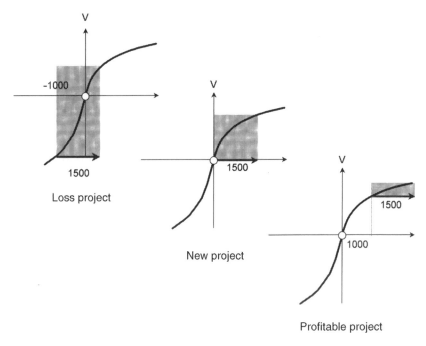

Figure 4-4   Effect of effort expended on three different projects.

Decreasing sensitivity and the evaluation of extreme losses or gains incurred

So far the discussion of relative evaluation has looked at expressions that are not too far removed from the reference point. We have showed the motives for risk-averse conduct in the profit zone and risk-taking behavior in the loss zone. However, there are often cases in which sensitivity in the value function increases again from a particular distance onwards, which has a direct effect on the attitude to risk (Kahneman and Tversky 1979). People in the loss zone will become risk-averse from a particular point onwards if we consider losses, for example, that are so high that they could have serious consequences on one's livelihood.

Take, for instance, a father who tries his luck in a casino in order to win the money for a fantastic family holiday. He will possibly risk some savings, and may even take out a loan if he has no luck at the start. As the head of a family, he will probably not be so irresponsible as to risk losing his family home, which he has only just been able to afford.

A different example shows a currency dealer who is authorized each day to trade only within a certain band. Let us assume he must consult his manager in order to get approval for any further trading in the case of a loss position of $200,000. The trader has got into trouble and must now decide whether he will realize a loss of $100,000 by clearing the position, or whether he will hold on to the position, with a 50 per cent probability of neutralizing his loss as well as a simultaneous 50 per cent risk that the loss will be increased to $200,000. The trader will probably act risk-averse from fear of embarrassment in front of his manager, realize the loss of $100,000 and then try to end the day in profit by trading cautiously. The relevant value function for this trader might well look something like that shown in Figure 4-5.

The value function shows that the trader becomes very sensitive in the vicinity of a loss of $200,000. Imagine a situation where two

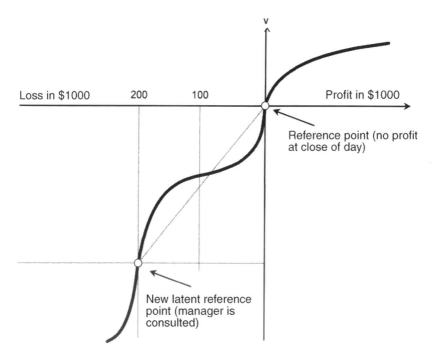

Figure 4-5   Risk aversion in the loss zone in the case of extreme expressions.

reference points play a role in the evaluation by the trader. One reference point is reaching close of trading without any profit. The second, at first only potential, reference point comes into play if sums in the vicinity of $200,000 must be evaluated. It should be noted that a decreasing sensitivity applies in the immediate vicinity of the two reference points. This is also plausible in the case of the second reference point, as the fact that this amount is exceeded or undercut is decisive.

It is easy to explain why the trader's behavior is risk-averse in the case of the value function in the decision-making situation related above. A loss of $200,000, as shown in the illustration, has a (negative) value that is more than doubled compared with a loss of $100,000. After multiplication with the 50 per cent probability, the total loss of $200,000 is still rated worse than the certain loss of $100,000 – the trader prefers the certain amount of loss.

Extreme expressions do not occur only in the loss zone; they can also be seen in the profit zone. Imagine someone who is fed up with his job and would like to get out. He buys lots of lottery tickets in order to win enough money to buy a small house in the Mediterranean and to lie on the beach for the rest of his life without any worries. His dream can only be realized with a certain amount of money. The value function will therefore also have a high sensitivity in the vicinity of the size of the gain in this case, analogous to the value function shown in Figure 4-5. Decreasing sensitivity is interrupted in this case, as the question of whether the would-be drop-out can fulfill his wish or not is decisive. The result is risk-taking behavior in the case of lotteries with a commensurate win.

These examples show clearly that the presence of additional reference points in the case of extreme expressions has something to do with the availability of objectives, which do not carry any weight in the case of decision making in "normal" examples. Only when goals in the profit zone approach feasible points, or danger-ous ones in the case of the loss zone, will they have a decisive effect on the evaluation of the total situation.

Relative evaluation in the light of mental accounting

The basic idea of mental accounting is that decision makers tend to debit costs associated with transactions to different "mental accounts", as explained earlier. A precondition is that these mental accounts are regarded independently of each other, i.e. each individual transaction is represented by its own account carried in the head (this often takes place subconsciously). The importance of mental accounting as an explanation for a number of typical behaviors, however, becomes clear only in the context of relative evaluation, as each of these mental accounts has its own reference point with an S-shaped value function (Tversky and Kahneman 1981).

Mental accounting is taken for granted in the examples above, as the basis was always the cost of individual projects (purchase of a particular share, repairs to a car etc.), but we showed only how decision-making behavior within an account is determined by reference points and decreasing sensitivity. The fact that this susceptibility can be categorized as incorrect behavior and lead to economic losses could be recognized, but this is easier to see when we look at several projects in parallel.

Economic disadvantages of the sunk cost effect
Imagine an entrepreneur who has started two ventures and "opened" mental accounts for them. Unfortunately, a loss of $1000 was incurred in the first project, while the other one produced a profit of $1000. The entrepreneur must now decide in which venture he will invest time and energy. The choice becomes even more difficult: it is assumed that he can only produce an additional $1500 in the case of the loss project (which has already incurred a sunk cost), while he will achieve an additional profit of $3000 for the same effort in the case of the profit project.

Figure 4-6 illustrates a configuration with decreasing sensitivity where the entrepreneur chooses the loss project because it will bring him a higher subjective increase in value than the doubled excess value in the profit project, despite the low extra value. We need not mention that this behavior results in a voluntary, yet irrational, sacrifice of $1500.

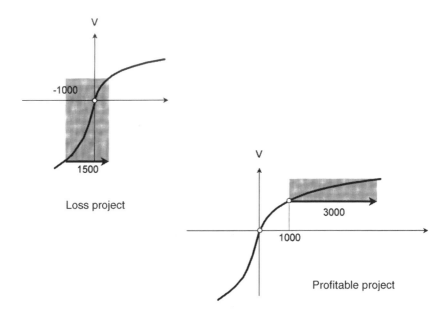

Figure 4-6   Increases in value in different mental accounts.

Economic disadvantages of decreasing sensitivity: the "liver sausage effect"

A man drives into town to choose a new cooker for his kitchen and at the same time buy four ounces of liver sausage for lunch. He goes first to store A, then visits store B. He likes one model that is offered by both stores. Store A offers the model at a price of $2480, $10 cheaper than the same model in store B. He decides to order the cooker from store B, even though it costs $10 more, because he is in a hurry and thinks, "Ten dollars won't make any difference."

Now imagine that the cookers are the same price in each store but that liver sausage costs $2 in store A and $6 in store B. Most people will decide to go back to the other store in this case. Although the man thought the $10 saving in the first case was not worth returning to store A for, he will go back for as little as $4 in the second case. We ask ourselves if it might not have been worthwhile to save $10 on the cooker after all.

The reason for this "liver sausage effect" would seem to be the interaction of mental accounting and decreasing sensitivity. While decreasing sensitivity in the cooker account when evaluating the cooker price results in the fact that the $10 is hardly noticed, this is not the case for the price of liver sausage. The difference between two dollars and six dollars is situated in the immediate vicinity of the reference point, which ensures high sensitivity.

Applied to a participant in the financial markets, this means that each individual exposure is considered in isolation. Each position therefore has its own mental account and a reference point, i.e. the cash price. The mental account is closed only with the final clearing of the exposure, whereby each profit or loss is transferred to a higher level "performance account", which is also kept in isolation and thus has its own reference point.

This can even result in the clearing of several exposures with small profits in order to sit out the loss of another position, i.e. to not have to realize the loss. The small profits are, individually, perceived relatively strongly, while a worsening of the loss position to the same amount will not have the same effect, due to decreasing sensitivity. This even occurs when economic or technical analyses urgently recommend hanging on to these positive exposures. The phenomenon of mental accounting is thus one of the main explanations for the behavior of market participants.

A similar effect occurs when exposures are entered on the basis of higher interest rates or other additional yields. For instance, currency A will be purchased against currency B because the interest level of currency A is considerably higher than that of currency B, i.e. the actor receives the difference in interest in respect of the two currencies while holding the position. These sums are transferred mentally to a separate account, independent of the basic position. We may assume that each individual payment of interest will be recorded individually, at least in the beginning (until one gets used to it). The less time between the receipt of the individual interest payments, the more mental accounts are "opened". As the reference point is situated at zero for each new account, these "profits" will be perceived as disproportionately great.

This contrasts with the mental account for the actual position, with the cost price as its reference point. There is no problem as long as this remains in the positive area. Things change, however, when the exposure moves into the loss zone, as we must then take into account the risk-taking behavior on the part of the actor.

Particularly in the case of large losses, when sensitivity declines sharply, mental accounting may lead to anything but pleasing results: additional losses are valued less than the profit of an individual interest account. The loss will therefore be realized even later than usual, as it is believed that the individual interest yields will largely compensate for the falling prices. Something similar applies to interest payments by the trader, which are also recorded mentally and individually. On the other hand, any profitable underlying position will be realized particularly early, as each individual charge weighs more than the perhaps still small profit arising from the underlying position.

Embellishment: another way of controlling several wins and losses
The various opportunities for creating mental accounts would suggest that there are different ways of arranging and keeping these accounts. This is usually based on the desire to see oneself in the best light possible when taking stock of all mental accounts, and to this end a number of mental transactions are undertaken between the individual balances. The term "hedonic framing"[5] is also used in this context. People deploy a reference frame that is attractive and in their favor, and that offers them the highest degree of satisfaction (Thaler and Johnson 1990, Linville and Fischer 1991, Hollenbeck et al. 1994).

We will explain this with the aid of an example. An investor has incurred a loss of $100 with exposure A, and a profit of $200 with exposure B. How can he account for these events mentally? On the one hand, he can keep an individual account in his head for each contract and thus simultaneously perceive a profit and a loss. This is called segregation. Decreasing sensitivity dictates that he is less pleased with the second $100 from exposure B than he is annoyed about the loss of $100 incurred by exposure A. The loss will be set off against part of the profit if he posts the exposures to a common account (integration), and the investor will perceive a total profit of $100. Integration of the two exposures therefore leads to a more attractive presentation, or to higher satisfaction (Thaler 1985).

Something similar occurs when several gains or losses must be

---

[5] Hedonism is the philosophy that has as its highest ethical principle the objective of satisfying the senses.

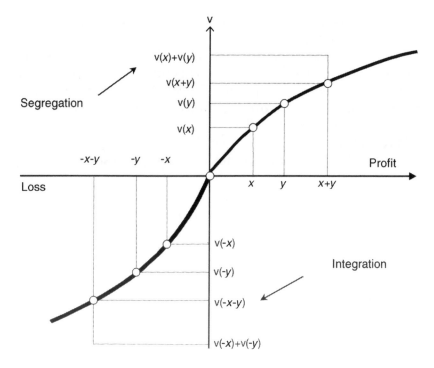

Figure 4-7   Integration and segregation in hedonic framing.

accounted for mentally. Figure 4-7 shows that it is more favorable to portray two gains (*x* and *y*) separately (segregation). On the other hand, losses must be presented as a totality (integration) in order to increase satisfaction (Thaler 1985).

These findings are exploited particularly in advertising and marketing. Take the case where a car is offered by a dealer at a price of $40,000. A similarly equipped car costs $45,000 from a different dealer, who offers several discounts totalling $5000. The final price therefore is also $40,000. A customer who has enquired at both dealers will most probably buy from the second dealer. The purchase of the car is set off against a single loss of $40,000 in the first case. The price of $45,000 in the second case will probably be perceived as a loss that is only slightly greater (due to decreasing sensitivity). The various discounts are, however, posted as profits to several accounts, and the customer feels better in the case of the second offer. This psychological effect is used by many dealers when determining prices and discounts (Herrmann and Bauer 1996, von Nitzsch 1998a).

Integration and segregation of gains and losses, however, can also be seen in a time context (Jungermann et al. 1998). For instance, if somebody has produced a very bad, possibly negative, return on their portfolio over a period of 12 months, then they are likely to combine this period with the possibly much more successful previous year as part of hedonic framing, i.e. they integrate the periods so that the overall position does not appear so bad after all.

Conclusion

At the start of this chapter, we described the typical process of evaluating situations. We showed how a particular reference point interacts with decreasing sensitivity to influence decision-making behavior. The location of the reference point was always plausible in the examples concerned. It was assumed, for instance, that a relative gain is always perceived when current wealth increases, while a loss is perceived when wealth decreases. The reference point is therefore determined by the current status quo.

This equation of the reference point with current wealth, however, cannot be generalized. We showed how reference points are moved easily by presenting the problem differently. There were, moreover, several reference points in the analysis of extreme expressions. It is easy to see why people change the reference points if it contributes to their sense of satisfaction (hedonic framing).

Let us take an investor as an example, who has acquired stock at a price of 50 euros. The share is quoted at 150 euros after a successful period of 12 months. Although the investor seriously considers selling the stock, he decides to continue with the exposure. Unfortunately, the ensuing period is characterized by one setback after another, and the investor will not sell because his reference point now stands at 150 euros, due not least to his deliberations when the share price reached its peak. Selling could therefore be seen as a relative loss in respect of this point. When he finally parts with the stock at a price of 70 euros, on the grounds of continued bad performance, he is quite happy. He has remembered his old reference point, the purchase price of 50 euros, in order to continue considering himself a winner: "I have still made 20 euros."

On the one hand, this example shows that it is difficult to define a single reference point. Usually this will be the purchase price, but individual intermediate prices that have a particular significance (e.g. a round listed price of 5000) may also be used as a reference point when commitments extend over a longer period of time. There are therefore several potential reference points. The more recent the relevant intermediate prices in question, the higher their availability for use as reference points and the sooner they are used for the evaluation.

On the other hand, it will be clear that the choice of reference points also depends to a large extent on personal characteristics. The investor described in the example was someone with a positive disposition, who was able to create satisfaction for himself through hedonic framing. A pessimist might well have got hung up on the peak price of 150 euros and might therefore have been confronted with a relative loss for some time.

It is not always easy to identify reference points. At the same time, we must not forget that there are clear factors that are not hard to assess. Market participants may bear in mind certain profit or yield targets that could function as reference points, in addition to the current state of their capital, which undoubtedly is an influential factor in relation to the reference point (Qualls and Puto 1989). An investor may, for instance, regard a yield achieved with high-risk stock as a relative loss if it is less than a secure investment might have yielded. A fund manager will talk about a relative loss when he performs worse than the market index. Similarly, an entrepreneur will perceive profit as a relative loss if it is below the profit of comparable companies in the same sector (Bowman 1980, Bowman 1982, Fiegenbaum and Thomas 1988). Thus expectation also plays a role in determining a reference point.

Moreover, plans or even firm intentions can also influence the reference point in a similar way. A person intent on changing their old car for a new one will usually have some idea of the cost and method of financing before their initial visit to the car dealer. Any subsequent evaluation of the actual cost is then no longer based on the current state of their wealth but will relate to the planned expenditure. They will be pleased with a relative gain should the car turn out to be cheaper than expected, while they will perceive a relative loss if the car is more expensive.

Before buying a car that you like, you need to collect sufficient information in order to plan the purchase. People will usually consider offers from competitors in the case of such an important decision, or they will recall past experiences (e.g. prices of recently bought cars). This means, in psychological terms, that people are already exposed to certain stimuli (in this case, prices) before facing a decision-making situation. We must assume that the reference point is determined by a particular level if all stimuli are situated at this same level. However, the reference point will take the form of a median value from the stimuli range in question if people are exposed to different stimulus levels.[6] The order of these stimuli is also relevant, of course (Lim 1995).

The salient point is that the reference point represents a value that must be regarded as "neutral" or "normal" in a certain sense. The stimuli that are considered normal by individuals depends on the current status quo, but also on expectations or plans that affect "normality".

RELATIVE EVALUATION OF PROBABILITY

We ought to assume that a decision maker evaluates a 50 per cent chance as a 50 per cent chance and a 50 per cent risk. But this is not always the case: quite different magnitudes of probability enter into the decision. The reason for this must be the phenomenon of a reduction in sensitivity at an increasing distance from the reference point. Sensitivity no longer depends on the personal situation, expectations and plans of the decision maker when estimating probability, but naturally stands at zero for losses or 100 per cent for gains (Tversky and Kahneman 1992). Because losses must

---

[6] Comprehensive experiments have shown that the adaptation level (i.e. the reference point in our terminology) can be determined quite well with the weighted geometric or logarithmic mean in the context of the adaptation level theory referred to earlier (Helson 1964). These findings are confirmed by Nwokoye (1975) and Antilla (1977) with their research into value-for-money judgments.

preferably occur not at all, gains should preferably occur with absolute certainty. A decision maker will consciously register a change in probability from 100 per cent to 99 per cent or from zero to one per cent, whereas a change in probability of, say, 43 per cent to 44 per cent will be overlooked by most decision makers.

There are two further interesting patterns of behavior in relation to probability, from which entire sectors of the economy benefit. Firstly, there is the "certainty effect", which poses that people value absolute certainty disproportionately high in relation to uncertain events. Anything that is uncertain is clearly valued less than certainty (Kahneman and Tversky 1979). Generally, the phrase "100 per cent probability is not as good as certainty" applies.

To portray this effect, imagine that you are playing Russian roulette. Ask yourself how much you would be prepared to pay for a single bullet in the gun instead of two. And what would you pay to have the last bullet removed? Undoubtedly more, unless you enjoy risking your life. Most people would pay quite a lot in order to buy certainty if their life depended on it.

The second characteristic is the overvaluation of small probabilities. The following two experiments illustrate this typically false estimation (Kahneman and Tversky 1979; the number of subjects who chose one of the alternatives is in brackets). You have a choice between a one-in-a-thousand chance of winning $5000 (72%) and a certain win of $5 (28%). Most people chose the risky alternative. Millions of people do the same when they buy a lottery ticket. Even when statistically knowledgeable friends demonstrate how small the chance of winning really is, they still have unconsciously higher values in mind and buy a lottery ticket at a price (based on the high turnover by lottery companies), which is considerably higher than the expectation value for winning. Who has never dreamed of what they could afford to do if they actually won? Many people are more than willing to pay a small price for this dream.

In the second game, you have a choice between a one-in-a-thousand risk of losing $5000 (17%) and a certain loss of $5 (83%). Most people make a risk-averse decision, as they estimate the risk of possibly losing $5000 as too high. The experiment makes clear in advance how high the risk is. However, this is not the case in many situations in daily life. The tendency to overestimate small risks in many areas of life is therefore even stronger. The insurance sector benefits from this phenomenon. How many liability policies are sold through this nightmare scenario? "Imagine that your dog runs out into the road and makes a tanker swerve ... petrol escaping everywhere ... seven million dollars' worth of damage!" An extremely rare but costly accident. The decision to buy insurance therefore amounts to weighing up the likelihood of a certain loss (insurance premium) against a very unlikely event (risk of the insured event).

HOW TIME AFFECTS JUDGMENT

In addition to the relative evaluation of probabilities, there is the different evaluation of action alternatives, depending on the time at which it takes place. The natural reference point is usually the present time – the here and now. Periods of time become increasingly less important as they are further removed from the present. The distinction as to whether something takes place today or tomorrow is perceived clearly. Most people will remain indifferent if an appointment in ten years' time is postponed by one day. Decreasing sensitivity at time level comes into play here. The time factor therefore also influences the way decision makers evaluate the result of an action. We must assume, for instance, that people would rather have something today than later – as a result the utility of a product is reduced if it becomes available later, i.e. if the use is discounted (Roelofsma and Keren 1995).

The economic consequences of this relative evaluation can also be shown by the "common difference effect" (Loewenstein and Thaler 1989, Loewenstein 1992). The following example taken from an experiment with students (Roelofsma and Keren 1995) will help explain this effect (the percentage of subjects who chose the alternative in each case is shown in brackets). Which of the following situations is preferable: receiving $100 today (82%) or receiving $110 in four weeks' time (18%)? In addition, you have a choice between $100 in 26 weeks' time (37%) and $110 in 30 weeks' time (63%).

Although a large majority decided on the immediate receipt

of $100 in the first case (even though a waiting period of four weeks would have been rewarded by interest paid at 10 per cent monthly), the time factor does not play a role in the case of the second choice. Yet the interval between the times at which payment would be received is the same in both cases. An economic and rational explanation of this effect might be possible in theory if the market was characterized by a rapidly dropping interest rate, or if the subjects had expected a higher rate of interest during the first four weeks than during the period following the 26 weeks. Allowing for the fact that the alternatives offered incorporate an annual rate of interest of more than 100 per cent, then this explanation can be discarded, as the subjects' opportunity interest would have to be even greater for the first four weeks. We therefore conclude that the fact that most of the subjects in the first comparison chose the $100 is a result of decreasing sensitivity.

The experiment also shows that the same period of time (four weeks) is not perceived as being of the same length. Rather, the sense of time depends on the distance to the reference point (the present time). The period of time will be undervalued the further it is removed from this reference point. Take a child, for example, who is looking forward to the summer holiday with his parents. The child will not mind much if the holiday is postponed by a fortnight from the middle to the end of July if he is told about the holiday in February, as they will not be going on holiday for several months. It is still quite far removed from the reference point "present" on the time axis. But the child might well be very disappointed to hear that the holiday has been postponed immediately before the planned start of the holiday, and the fortnight's wait will seem an eternity.

The similarity to the certainty effect, which poses that decision makers prefer absolute certainty to an extent that is disproportionally strong compared with probability, however high, now becomes clear. As far as time is concerned, this corresponds to a disproportionate preference for immediate events compared with events that will occur after a period of time. We will therefore call the "immediacy effect". It explains why the majority of subjects in the test group preferred the immediate receipt of $100.

Chapter 5

People like to see themselves in a favorable light

The consequences of psychological needs

The weaknesses in perception, processing and the evaluation of information discussed in Chapters 3 and 4 are based on physiological factors. We explained the mechanisms people use to process information in order to overcome the complexity of decision-making situations and to arrive quickly at judgments, handicapped by a capacity limited by nature. Finally, the effects of the phenomenon of relative evaluation were discussed in Chapter 4.

This chapter deals with weaknesses, in particular in perception and evaluation, which are the result of particular psychological needs. We focus on two main motives. Everybody likes to control their own situation and immediate surroundings as much as possible, and people also like to be able to refer to a logical system of opinions, beliefs and knowledge. It will be clear that the first motive presupposes the second one, for control based on contradictory observations, opinions, knowledge, convictions and attitudes (so-called cognitions) would hardly seem possible.

A NEED FOR HARMONY: YEARNING TO BE FREE OF DISSONANCE

Everybody has asked themselves, at some time, whether they have made the right decision, or whether the alternative would have been better. Such thoughts crop up in many situations in everyday life. Imagine you have been invited out to dinner by your boss. You are in the restaurant with your colleagues and are the first to choose from the menu. It would not be good form to choose the most expensive dish, but the cheapest will not do either. You end up choosing something from the middle of the menu, say veal with Calvados sauce. The other orders are taken one by one, and the "courage" of the other guests to order dishes that are a little more expensive increases. Then it is the host's turn, and he decides on saddle of venison Baden-Baden, the high point of the menu. Immediately, you regret your choice, because you would have preferred game, but wouldn't it have seemed greedy to choose the venison? Now you regret being so modest, and you are in a bad mood before the meal is even served.

There are theoretically two possibilities to escape from this dilemma. One of these is to change your mind and simply order something else. This is, however, out of the question if you are part of a group, for you would not like to give your host – who is also your boss – the impression that you are indecisive or even greedy. The second possibility is easier and more discreet: match your perception to your decision. This could be done by extolling your own choice: isn't it the best veal you have tasted for a long time? Or you could deride the alternative that you declined: doesn't the venison look a bit on the dark side, even a little burnt? Perhaps it is tough. And the side dishes don't look very appetizing either. Just as well you didn't choose it.

An actor in the financial markets could behave similarly, having decided to purchase stock x, but wondering whether the purchase of a different share might not have been better. The decision could be reversed by selling share x, although this would incur transaction costs. He would also make a loss too if the share price fell. As the investor in this situation might find it very difficult to sell the share, he will look for reasons and information to justify the original decision. Information that runs counter to the purchase of the share will be ignored as far as possible. This behavior is explained in psychology with the aid of cognitive dissonance theory, which is based on the work of the psychologist Leon Festinger (1957).

Cognitive dissonance theory

A conflict arises after nearly all decisions involving a choice between alternatives. This is because the chosen alternative often has negative aspects, and the rejected alternative also has positive characteristics. The characteristics or information contradicts the opinion of the decision maker, who is convinced he has made the best possible choice. Such a contradiction is known as "cognitive dissonance" in psychology. The word "cognitive" is derived from the word "cognition", which in general means any form of conscious process (units of information, belief or knowledge). We speak of a consonant relationship if these cognitions agree with one another; if they contradict one another, then we speak of a dissonant relationship.

A fundamental premise in cognitive dissonance theory is that all people try to resolve any conflict between perception and thinking as soon as possible, as conflicts are experienced as unpleasant. How is this done? We manipulate individual cognitions in such a way that they match all others.

Let's look again at the example of the restaurant. A decision was made in favor of veal in a Calvados sauce. All cognitions contradicting this choice will create cognitive dissonance. These are the positive characteristics of the alternative that was not chosen, i.e. the delighted expression on the face of your boss as he tastes the venison, and also the aroma of the game as it reaches your nostrils. The dissonance increases even more if the veal does not taste as good as expected, when, in addition, the chosen alternative proves to have negative characteristics. In order to resolve this depressing sensation, cognitions are sought that are consonant with the decision taken. One might think for instance, "Yes, this is the best veal I have had for a long time." Another possibility is to change dissonant cognitions into consonant ones. The "crisply cooked saddle of venison" then becomes "a little burnt"; the "delicious aroma of the cooked game" becomes a "slightly musty smell". In addition, dissonant cognitions can be ignored by looking the other way.

Two situations play an important role in the generation of consonance and dissonance. Firstly, only observations that have a "relevant" relationship and that are perceived by the decision maker are important (Beckmann 1984), i.e. they must attract attention. There is, for example, no relevant relationship between the following cognitions or observations: "the veal kidney looks delicious" and "the waiter has a bowtie".

Secondly, a particular "commitment" is a prerequisite for the creation of dissonance. Commitment occurs when we have an emotional attachment to a decision (Brehm and Cohen 1962). The stronger the attachment, or the greater the commitment, the stronger the dissonance. Without commitment there is no dissonance. The example of the restaurant includes such a commitment, as the individual enjoyed looking through the menu and chose the veal kidney apparently voluntarily, and is therefore responsible for his choice. Reversing the decision would mean that one was indecisive or even greedy in the eyes of his boss, so he had no alternative but to stand by his decision.

Reasons for the existence of commitment when making a decision

The extent of the commitment, and therefore the possible dissonance, in the case of a particular decision depends on four factors: freedom to choose, irreversible cost, accountability and departure from the norm.[1]

Freedom to choose
Research into dissonance theory has shown that dissonance can arise only if a decision has been taken voluntarily, i.e. a free choice has been made from at least two alternatives (Frey and Gaska

---

[1] Brehm and Cohen (1962) regard freedom of choice, in addition to commitment, as an independent condition for the creation of dissonance. They also have a more restricted view of commitment than the one presented here.

1998). If your boss tells you to carry out a particular action, then there is no question of commitment, and there is no emotional attachment to the decision. The boss will be responsible if the outcome is not as expected. If you were not allowed to choose from the menu in the restaurant example because the boss had ordered for everyone in advance, then the commitment would be minimal, and there would be no conflict.

Commitment in the financial markets will, on the other hand, always be very high, as normally nobody is compelled to invest. Rather, the decision to invest is entirely voluntary. The trader who merely executes an order for a client will not experience dissonance.

Accountability

A distinction must be made when assigning accountability as to whether people are accountable to themselves or to others. Basically, commitment to a decision will increase in line with accountability in both cases. Much depends on how the accountability is perceived (Wicklund and Brehm 1976).

A precondition for the attribution of accountability is that the consequences of the action must, to a certain extent, have been predictable. In other words, it must be obvious, at least after the event, that a development could have been foreseen (Goethals et al. 1979). Most fund managers would feel responsible to only a limited extent for losses resulting from surprising, unpredictable political events (e.g. a coup). The responsibility is played down if the political events could have been foreseen. Most people will tend to blame their failure on their surroundings in that case.

We see that positive results, on the other hand, are ascribed to one's own skills, and in this case people are only too willing to accept full responsibility (e.g. Pyszczynski and Greenberg 1987). No fund manger would shy away from claiming responsibility for gains on the stock exchange, even if these resulted from abnormal and unexpected events. People like to think they had foreseen the movement – after all, that is why they took that position.

The fundamental attribution error is important where accountability to others is concerned. As already stated, it consists of the fact that the absence of success, or the failure of an action, is based on the skill or failure on the part of the actor, rather than on the conditions and circumstances of his action. We must always take into account that others (prematurely) ascribe the responsibility for decisions to us, if our decisions touch on their interests. This occurs even when factors that one clearly could not have foreseen or controlled influence the outcome of an affair. A fund manager who enters a long position shortly before a political event that causes prices to fall sharply will be judged incompetent by investors. If he sold a large percentage of the shares in question shortly before, for whatever reason, then he is said to have a good feel for the market, and people will entrust their money to him even more in future. This phenomenon causes decision makers to be particularly committed whenever others – even if only as observers – are involved in their actions. This applies in particular to fund managers or administrators, as the results of their actions always affect vital interests of third parties (investors in shares or investment funds).

Irreversible cost of the decision or cost involved in reversing a decision
The commitment also includes costs incurred as a result of a decision, which cannot be reclaimed. This also represents a sunk cost. It results in a high commitment, as do costs that are incurred at the time the decision is actually reversed.

But we are not only dealing with real cost, such as the cost of repairs in the case of a car, or a drop in the price of a share. Many decisions also extract a psychological price – for instance, when it takes a lot of time and effort to consider a situation until your mind is finally made up (Zimbardo 1965). When you finally decide on a particular action after protracted consideration of the matter, then you will find it far from easy to reverse the decision. The expression, "I am set on …" makes clear what is involved. So we see that not only the decision, but also the firm intention formed in the mind to decide one way or another, can give rise to dissonant feelings.

Departure from the norm
The more an action departs from the norm, the greater the commitment. On the other hand, decisions that conform to the norm involve much less commitment. "Normal" in this context signifies what a large majority in the environment of the actor does

or thinks is right, irrespective of whether it actually is right or wrong. Take, for instance, the introduction of the euro in 1999, which was greeted almost with euphoria by politicians and economists in all countries. Who would have dared build up a short position in euros against the opinion of a majority of experts? A sale of euros (e.g. against the dollar) would have meant a considerable departure from the norm in this situation, when the majority was convinced of the stability of the euro: it would have involved a considerable commitment. And if the price of the euro had risen, as the majority expected, then dissonance would have presented many problems.

The norm theory defines which decisions are ultimately regarded as normal and which are deviating from the norm (Kahneman and Miller 1986).[2] Normal is what is easily conceivable, and anything that is hard to imagine departs from the norm. Considering that the immediate situation or the present development is easiest to imagine, for reasons of availability, then decisions that preserve the status quo are held to be "normal". Measures deviating from the norm are those that lead to a change in the current situation or development. So, when a decision is made that departs from the status quo, then the person in question forms a particular and more prominent relationship with this decision, i.e. there is a higher commitment than in the case of a "normal" decision. Should such a decision turn out to be wrong, then it will give rise to strong feelings of dissonance. For this reason, decisions that deviate from the norm are frequently avoided. Think of a football trainer who sticks with his proven team before an important game, rather than giving young, promising players a chance.

This phenomenon can also be seen in the financial markets. Many investors tend to include blue-chip shares in their portfolio, corresponding to a "normal" investment strategy. Investing in small, unknown companies (which might show a higher growth potential), on the other hand, represents a departure from the norm, and is accompanied by a high commitment (De Bondt and Thaler 1995). Losses or gains will therefore be evaluated higher than in the case of blue-chip shares.

---

[2] According to norm theory, the stimulus that activates most cognitive elements is the norm.

Consequences of the need to be free of dissonance

Dissonance is experienced as an unpleasant state that people try to avoid or, if this is impossible, at least to reduce in intensity. Most people will try to avoid dissonant situations, and they will try to avoid, or even ignore, information that might increase their discomfort. According to Festinger, cognitive dissonance is similar to a state of tension, comparable to a basic drive, such as hunger, that must be removed or satisfied. The stronger the dissonance, the stronger the urge to reduce it – the greater the hunger, the stronger the desire to eat as much as possible.

There are several possibilities to remove or reduce dissonance. To reduce dissonance by reversing a decision already taken, you must overcome internal and external obstacles. Such a measure could incur not only cost but also mental distress. Take a graduate student who thinks he has finally found his dream job, which pays him a generous salary. If, after a while, he finds it very difficult to live up to expectations, he could hand in his notice and find a new occupation that suits him better. The decision is a difficult one. He has spent a long time looking for this job – should he now give it up, just like that? And his parents would be very disappointed, because they were so proud when he told them what a good job he had found. Nor would he like to admit such a defeat to himself. Not to mention the effort that a change of job would entail. And who guarantees that there won't be any problems in the new company? He might end up worse off.

The fear that a change could mean the loss of advantages will also lessen the willingness to reverse a decision once made. The graduate considers the atmosphere at his current job excellent; he has also made friends amongst his new colleagues, and would sorely miss the cooperation with them. And the pay is very good. A change of job would therefore mean giving up these consonant cognitions.

But often it is simply impossible to reverse a decision. Say you have just sold your dream car and would like to buy it back immediately after, but the new owner will not sell the car for all the money in the world. If there is no chance of reversing the decision, either because of high commitment or simply because it is impossible, then dissonance must be resolved in another way. There are two possibilities: selective perception and selective decisions.

Selective perception

Selective perception is the phenomenon in which people register only what puts their decision in a favorable light if the decision was accompanied by a high commitment. They do this mainly when the signs that the decision was actually unfavorable multiply (Frey 1981a). In such a situation, attention is drawn to the advantages of the chosen alternative, as well as to the disadvantages of the rejected possibility; people therefore observe mainly information in favor of the decision made. Contradictory information is preferably ignored, or at least played down as far as the consequences are concerned. Consider the following ad hoc announcement by a company:

Turnover and profit targets still achievable!

Turnover as well as profits have fallen during the last quarter, due to continued sharp competition. The management hopes to take steps that will still allow for the projected turnover and profit targets to be realized.

What information would you, as the holder of several shares in this company, pay particular attention to, and what would you play down or even ignore?

The fact that distorted perception increases well-being is surely a positive aspect. Use of this subconscious automatism helps to realize the desire to be free of dissonance without changing reality. This self-protection phenomenon becomes problematic only when further decisions must be made (Stahlberg et al. 1998). In this case, the person will refer to information available but will distort it in order to meet a need. It is obvious that this might give rise to wrong decisions. The investor in the above example remembers only that the company still hopes to achieve its turnover and profit targets. The investment still makes sense to him, especially since he recalls that the profit targets were high anyway and that the shares were recommended as a buy as recently as eight months ago. He sees a subsequent drop in price as a good opportunity to buy, so he increases his investment. Once he recognizes that he has ignored the sharp competition and price war for too long, or has played it down, it will be too late.

The tendency to selective perception is not equally strong in all people. Two groups can be distinguished: those with closed minds and those with open minds. The first group relates to people who experience dissonance as bad and consistently strive for consonance (consistency seekers). They therefore risk persisting with wrong decisions or acting wrongly in new situations due to a biased selection of information.

Open-minded people are more like Earnest Coldheart. Although they also strive for consonance, they are normally prepared to cope with dissonant cognitions on the way. They will, for instance, carefully read the ad hoc announcement. They will note that the company is confronted with a difficult price war, which may entail considerable problems for the future. They will also recognize that the management only hopes to be able to take counter measures. If these messages all speak against a further investment, then they are willing to admit that the decision to invest was a wrong one, and they will consider selling their shares.

Individuals with a closed mind also cope to some extent with dissonant cognitions, but only when they believe they can refute them logically and without much difficulty (Frey 1981b). Interestingly, dissonant information is often sought out consciously by many people. This happens when they believe they can easily refute it. They might, for instance, search the papers for information that contradicts their personal opinion or even a decision just made, but that is illogical or obviously badly researched. They will happily tear to pieces such articles, at the same time robbing dissonant information of its right of existence. Would the same decision maker be just as critical about a consonant piece of information? Probably not.

Selective decision making

Whereas selective perception serves to justify a decision, or to reduce dissonance, people making selective decisions will act in such a way that their initial decision, probably accompanied by high commitment, leads to the desired result in any case, even if they must pay a high price for this. They will continue to invest in a project, hoping that the investment so far has not been for nothing. There are many examples of such considerations. Take the many battles, which, though long since lost, are continued with the same determination in the hope of being victorious in the end. This behavior can also be seen in stock markets, of which the collapse of Barings is an impressive example. Hoping to drive the Japanese stock market in the "right" direction, Nick Leeson gambled every-thing – and lost. Investors who watch the price of shares they have bought drop continuously will act in a similar fashion, albeit on a smaller scale. Hoping to arrive in the profit zone soon, they will invest more and more capital in the stock in order to reduce the initial purchase price. At some point, they will become frustrated and give up, having possibly lost a large part of their capital if the price continues to fall.

Selective decision making is ultimately nothing more than a detailed version of the disposition or sunk cost effect, which we introduced in the previous chapter on relative evaluation. Dissonance theory tells us that not only irreversible costs as part of the interaction with a relative evaluation, but rather all factors that lead to a high commitment associated with decisions, might result in holding on to loss-making projects. The extent of the accountability, as well as a possible departure from the norm in particular, must be taken into account. High commitment accompanying a decision may therefore reinforce the already dangerous sunk cost effect.

Dissonance anticipation in evaluations

The desire to avoid dissonance can have a sustained effect on per-ception and decisions. Many people consider, either consciously or subconsciously, whether their decisions might lead to dissonance in the future, insofar as they are able to foresee possible negative consequences (which therefore might give rise to dissonance) (Wicklund and Brehm 1976). As a result, alternatives that lead to the least dissonance are usually chosen.

Loss aversion
Numerous studies have shown that people feel losses more deeply than gains of the same value (Kahneman and Tversky 1979, Tversky

and Kahneman 1991). People are therefore more annoyed about a loss of $100 than they are pleased with a profit of $100. This phenomenon is called "loss aversion". It can be explained with the aid of dissonance theory. As losses obviously imply that a decision was wrong, they give rise to dissonance, which puts the decision maker under pressure to justify the decision, which then invokes a psychological cost. There is no question of a psychological cost in the profit area, which explains the asymmetry in the evaluation of profits and losses. Loss aversion can be depicted with the value function deployed in prospect theory, similar to relative evaluation. It then becomes clear that the value curve is much steeper in the loss area than in the profit area. Dissonance, or the drive to remove dissonance, depends on the commitment of the trader to his decision, as we have shown. This means that the degree of loss aversion depends directly on commitment. Figure 5-1 illustrates this effect.

The degree of loss aversion can be measured against the reference point in particular. The enlargement of the immediate area

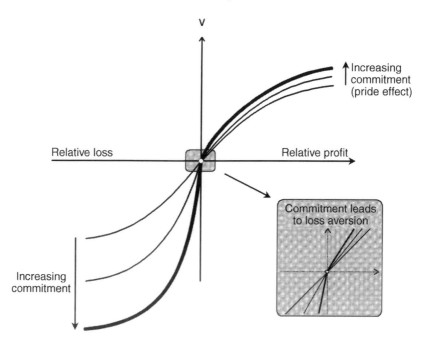

Figure 5-1   Relationship between commitment and loss aversion.

around the reference point shows that the curve of the value function around the reference point in the profit and the loss zones is identical without commitment, so there is no loss aversion. This would be the case, for example, for a loss arising from a decision one is forced to make (e.g. a robbery in which one is forced to hand over the money, or a tax increase against which one cannot appeal). Loss aversion grows with increased commitment, i.e. the value function is clearly steeper in the loss zone, the commitment being equal in both zones.

Taking into account that any departure from the norm (i.e. a conscious departure from the present situation) leads to a commitment, then loss aversion also plays a role when weighing up a decision that changes the status quo. This will give rise to a further important effect – the "endowment effect".

The endowment effect (Thaler 1980), also known as "status quo bias" (Samuelson and Zeckhauser 1988), is the phenomenon in which most people would demand a considerably higher price for a product that they own than they would be prepared to pay for it (Weber 1993). This effect has been identified in numerous experiments, and is also seen frequently in everyday life. Take a valuable heirloom that has been through a lot. The parents of the inheritor have already regaled to him how it saved his grandfather's life during the war, placed in the breast pocket over his heart: a bullet was deflected by the lid of the watch. When a friend admires the heirloom and asks how much he would be willing to sell the pocket watch for, the owner answers proudly, "Not less than $5000," even though the antiquarian around the corner would not be willing to pay more than $500 for the same watch.

A similar effect was achieved by one of the authors when he offered to sell a lottery ticket worth $20 for a draw held the following weekend to one of the attendees at a presentation. At the same time, he asked the buyer to try and commit the seven-digit number to memory. The attendee was willing to swap the lottery ticket for another only when offered $40 for it. Most subjects in a similar experiment behaved in the same way (Knetsch and Sinden 1984).

We could argue, of course, that this behavior is completely rational. We would all like to sell things at a profit – if we want to sell them at all. However, in all these cases the difference between the buying and the selling price is so high that it cannot be explained by greed alone. It became clear, for instance, that the owner of the watch, the attendee at the presentation, and the subjects in the experiment strongly identified with their goods, i.e. they all showed a high commitment. In the case of the heirloom in particular, a certain responsibility towards the deceased person, as well as a considerable departure from the norm, would have played a role. There is possibly also the thought that the watch might save the inheritor's own life in future, just as it saved his grandfather's. Committing the lottery ticket number to memory had the effect of a commitment, due to the psychological cost (anger and regret) that might arise if the lottery ticket, once sold, was drawn the following week. Moreover, deliberately changing the situation by selling the lottery ticket would entail a departure from the norm, leading to a rise in commitment and therefore dissonance.

The endowment effect is explained with the aid of Figure 5-2, which compares two situations: the sale of a particular product and a subsequent further sale of the same product.[3] The buyer in the purchase situation perceives the acquisition of the product as a profit in the mental account opened for the occasion. This leads to an increase in value of x. Considering the maximum price he is prepared to pay, he needs to look for a sum equalling a negative value of x representing the loss in the mental "money" account. This amount is the maximum purchase price. The reference points are different in the sale situation. The disposal of the good represents a loss, leading to a negative value of y. The receipt of the selling price in the "money" account represents a profit. The minimum selling price can be calculated in the same way as the purchase price; it becomes clear that it is considerably higher than the maximum purchase price (see also Tversky and Kahneman 1991). The cause of the endowment effect in this example lies solely in the loss aversion in the two mental accounts.

The endowment effect is also called "status quo bias", defined as the tendency to leave everything as it is. This inclination is so strong because the disadvantages of changing tried and tested methods are felt more strongly than the advantages that might accrue upon changing these achievements. Why would people

---

[3]   We assume that the reference point represents the actual status quo in each case, i.e. the purchase or sale in this case is not fixed.

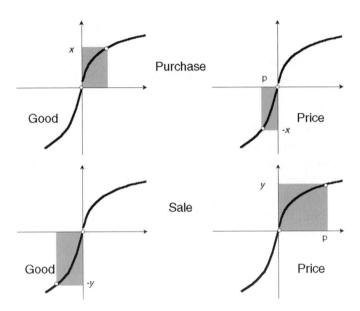

Figure 5-2   The endowment effect.

depart from methods that, although not perfect in the past, have yielded a certain, consistent result year after year? It is therefore relatively difficult for people to take an innovative route – unless the new ideas promise considerably more success than the old ones. This also gives rise to brand loyalty amongst consumers. Why change the toothpaste with which you have been cleaning your teeth for years?

Manufacturers also exploit the endowment effect when inviting customers to try out products (von Nitzsch 1998a) or when giving them away, for example a newspaper delivered free for a fortnight before the subscription becomes due, or an expensive luxury car that the sales manager lets you try out free for the weekend, although you originally only wanted to buy a car in the medium price range. When you are subsequently handed the keys on the Friday, it will be booked mentally as a profit, although you know that the car will have to be returned again.[4] Returning the luxury limousine to the dealer on Monday morning will be perceived as a mental loss. The car has not changed but the loss on the Monday is

---

[4]   More precisely, the difference between the price that one would have paid originally for the car (reference point) and the increased value will be booked as a profit.

heavier than the mental profit on the Friday. This phenomenon is responsible for the fact that many people ultimately decide to buy the car after a similar test weekend, despite the fact that there was no intention to buy a posh car in the first place.

Regret aversion

This is a further behavior anomaly. Regret aversion is the endeavor to not make any wrong decisions in order to avoid regret or disappointment. People regard many decisions from the point of view of "What would have happened if I had made a different decision?" The disappointment in the case of a wrong decision might outweigh the joy had the decision been successful (Loomes and Sugden 1982, Loomes and Sugden 1987, Loomes 1988). The easier it is to imagine what would be the right step, the more one regrets doing the "wrong thing" (Kahneman and Tversky 1982). The results of a wrong decision are perceived as more negative than the damage that might be incurred through doing nothing. This leads people to be passive rather than active, insofar as they are confronted with decision-making situations under uncertain conditions, and to rely on the old ways instead.

A market participant whose investment has gone into the loss zone will therefore hesitate to realize this loss, because he risks getting out at the most unfavorable point. In that case, he would not only have incurred a loss, but would also lose face because this would prove that the first decision – to open a position – was wrong. The second decision – liquidating a position – could entail emotional consequences that are worse than those following the first decision. If the exposure is liquidated at the worst point, then this could mean that the first decision was possibly correct after all. But the trader would have obviously been incapable of using the opportunity, and has instead fallen victim to his feelings of panic. He will lose face even more if this error is witnessed by others (Shefrin and Statman 1985).

On the positive side, pride (the opposite of regret aversion, also called "pride effect") may cause profit to be realized too soon. Profits that can be attributed to a person as a success are evaluated more highly than gains caused by circumstances only. This effect will also be stronger in the presence of witnesses, because there is public proof that a correct decision was made.

This also explains why market participants with an unfavorable position look to justify their actions with "old" information (which was decisive for an earlier decision) (Beeler and Hunton 1997) – they wish to share, or even completely shift, the responsibility. In extreme cases they will say, "The others agreed with me at the time, so I can't be that stupid," or "Speculators are to blame for my loss." Yet most people will always claim full responsibility for gains. Allegedly, they did not need to call on analysts or information provided by a third party. Blaming someone else, however, also means reducing the commitment and therefore the dissonance that accompanies the decision.

If regret aversion signifies the fear of regretting decisions after the event (Loomes and Sugden 1982, Loomes and Sugden 1987), then what is the difference compared with loss aversion? The difference becomes clear when we remember that regret may also occur when a particular decision has not been made. Had we, for instance, not bought a particular share, against the advice of a friend, and the share then turns out to be a winner, then regret kicks in, even though there was no actual loss. Not acting is a decision – you choose to not act.

The difference between loss aversion and regret aversion becomes even clearer if we imagine two different classes of mental account. On the one hand, there are "payment effect" mental accounts to which the actual money is booked. (So far, we have always based our discussions on mental accounting on this type of account.) On the other hand, people also keep "non-payment effect" mental accounts, which record those sums that might have been received if a particular decision had not been made, which means that these payments do not affect the actual state of the capital (Figure 5-3).

For instance, if you sell a share that subsequently increases in value, then you will keep on calculating the profit that you would have made if you had hung on to the share. You will undoubtedly think, "How stupid of me, I would now be $20,000 richer if I hadn't sold those shares." Similarly, many investors also calculate the loss they would have incurred if they had not sold the shares, for instance immediately before a downward trend: "Lucky I acted in time, otherwise I might have lost $50,000." The precondition for a non-payment effect account is merely the fact that it is possible

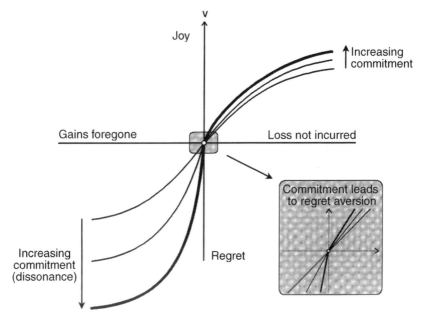

Figure 5-3   Regret aversion in the case of a non-payment effect account.

to calculate the success or failure resulting from the alternative that was not chosen.

Gains foregone take the place of a loss in the case of evaluation of a non-payment effect project; the relative gain, on the other hand, will be replaced by the loss not incurred. Dissonance occurs when the decision against the project is regretted because it would have produced a profit. The degree of regret aversion, as with loss aversion, can be seen from the increase in the non-payment effect "regret function" in the vicinity of the reference point. The dissonance is great and the regret aversion pronounced if the decision against the project was accompanied by considerable commitment. As with loss aversion, a decision maker anticipates the dissonance when considering the realization of a particular project (Loomes and Sugden 1982, Loomes and Sugden 1987).

For instance, an investor acquires shares at a price of 100 euros. Unfortunately, the price barely moves for a long time, and the investor wonders whether it would not be better to sell. Many people have advised him to sell the shares, yet he has not done so. He thinks, "If I sell the shares today, and the price suddenly rises, as I have long been expecting, then I would be really annoyed" (regret aversion). The investor identifies closely with his shares, due to the extended period he has held this investment, so the decision is associated with considerable commitment. This commitment would be even stronger if the investor decided on the sale and therefore would depart from the status quo (and also the norm). A subsequent missed profit will be experienced as particularly painful in this case. The reasons are not particularly rational: a decision to hold on to a share should not depend on the fact that one might be annoyed if the price would start to rise the moment one had decided to sell the stock.

The situation is quite different for an investor who has only superficially taken note of the share price and who has decided against the purchase without a prior detailed analysis. This investor may also follow further price movements. He might even be annoyed should the share price suddenly jump, but the magnitude of his regret would not be the same as in the case of the first investor, as his decision not to buy would be accompanied by a small commitment.

Managing loss and regret aversion
The concept of loss aversion indicates the phenomenon that losses are valued significantly higher after decisions with a high commitment than losses following decisions with a minimal commitment. This phenomenon is economically irrational, as is shown by the following example.

A lottery ticket seller offers a finance officer, well-known for his thrift, a gamble: he risks losing $100 with a 50 per cent probability, but he may win $150 with a similar probability. A quick glance at the possible gain and loss makes him consider it, but he declines the offer resolutely for he is not a gambler. Returning home, he finds a letter from a lottery company inviting him to play the following game: a 50 per cent risk of losing $100 against a 50 per cent chance of winning $140. The finance officer feels lucky, writes a cheque and posts it immediately.

Both bets are identical, but the win is ten dollars less in the second case. So why does the finance officer, who must surely be good at math, respond to the second offer, after he resolutely turned down the first one? He felt that he was watched in the first case and, as a municipal officer, he had a reputation to lose. The fact that the cautious administrator of the municipal coffers might be involved in a lottery game would be equal to a glaring departure from the norm. There are no witnesses to his participation in the lottery in the second case: nobody would be any the wiser after a loss, so his commitment is clearly less in this case. This decision-making behavior is, of course, irrational from an economic point of view.

Conduct becomes economically rational only when the commitment has no influence on the evaluation and decision-making behavior. Everybody should first try to estimate how high their commitment is, i.e. consider whether any sunk costs have already incurred, or whether the imminent decision signifies a departure from the norm, in order to make a rational decision. The higher the commitment that accompanies the decision, the greater the risk that possible negative results will be overestimated. In other words, one's capacity for judging is limited, and the perception of the situation is distorted. Only those who are aware of this can correct these errors.

If, on the other hand, there is agreement that a commitment a priori leads to distortions and therefore that all decisions must be made free from any commitment as far as possible, then any problems arising from regret aversion will be resolved of their own accord. In order to be able to make decisions free from regret or loss aversion in the financial markets, people should try to keep their own commitments to a minimum. The most important influential factor, sunk cost, can be circumvented by, for example, trying to forget one's purchase price, for people tend to calculate their losses and to hold on to the investment only until they are in the profit zone. All associated problems can be avoided in this way. Hold on to a share only if you would currently also invest in the share (if it was not already held).

BETTING ON A CERTAINTY: THE NEED TO CONTROL

A strong desire to control is not the prerogative of obsessional people. Nobody likes to be without power, exposed to the inconstancy of fate and the arbitrariness of others, helpless and without any opportunity to control things. The urge to control is particularly obvious in the financial markets, where winners and losers appear everyday. The trick here is to be one step ahead of the majority of market participants, to use the movements of the markets through strategies, techniques and successful analyses and thus to become one of the winners. This section will explain that the control motive is a significant psychological basic need.

The importance of the motive to control

The theoretical concept of the control motive (White 1959, DeCharms 1968) assumes that every person has the need to perceive himself as the originator of changes in his environment. This gives rise to feelings of competence and a sense of one's own value, so that the esteem afforded by others is influenced positively. Loss of control can have serious negative effects on well-being, as shown in numerous studies. These experiments show that an unfulfilled need for control can contribute to considerable negative mental effects, for example mice injected with cancer cells showed a significant increase in the cancer when exposed to uncontrollable negative stimuli (Sklar and Anisman 1981). It was also shown that terminally ill cancer patients who were moved to a hospice lived longer if they had been moved from another institution rather than directly from their homes (Schulz and Aderman 1973). Researchers attributed this effect to the fact that the patients in the second case suffered increased loss of control, which had a negative effect on the course of the disease.

A further study investigated to what extent an unpleasant jamming sound impedes solving a task that requires concentration (Glass and Singer 1972). The researchers formed two groups. The first group could not switch off the noise, and the second group could switch the noise off at any time. The leaders of the experiment asked the second group to complete the task without switching off, if possible. Significantly better results in the task requiring concentration were achieved by the second group, even without switching off the jamming sound. It would seem that not only the sound but also the lack of control – being at the mercy of something – affected the capacity to concentrate in the first group.

The theory of learned helplessness (Seligman 1975; Abramson et al. 1978) concerns the effect of a relatively long period of being at the mercy of something or someone. The perception of a lack of control invokes three effects: the need for control decreases, the ability to recognize relationships between effects decreases, and there will be fear, which may change into depression as certainty about the lack of influence increases (Osnabrügge et al. 1998). Applied to the financial markets, we may assume that investors who have experienced the fact that foreign and stock exchanges cannot be controlled in the long term withdraw from it and cease ...ng for a relatively long period (Bungard and Schulz-Gambard).

Forms of control

The "locus of control" (Rotter 1966) signifies the extent to which people anchor control in themselves (internal control) or perceive their fate to be manipulated by others or by blind forces (external control). According to this theory, successful people in particular have an internal locus of control, while "losers" often believe that they can do nothing to improve their situation. Their bad luck is blamed on others; life is against them and treats them badly.

We will explain first what we mean by "internal control", and we will introduce five variants of control. The first shows the strongest form of control – control decreases with each following variant. It does not matter for the purposes of meeting the need for control whether people actually control the situation or whether they only *think* they do. This means that the experienced, perceived control (also called "cognitional control") is described, rather than the actual control (Osnabrügge et al. 1998). In other words, people have a need to be convinced that they have control.

Control through influence

People who are under the impression that they are able to influence the course of things to a considerable extent experience the strongest form of control, which also fully meets the need for control. A typical example is the millions of car drivers for whom their own vehicle is a symbol of freedom, and who also consider themselves to be masters of the situation in most circumstances if they are the drivers. Steering the car gives them a secure feeling and the sense that they will be able to avert a possible accident, as they are confident that they can respond quickly. In contrast, they must rely on the driving ability of others in taxis, trains or airplanes. The feeling of being at the mercy of someone else is probably greatest in airplane passengers – perhaps the fear of flying is partly due to this lack of control.

We must assume that investors in the financial markets generally do not have any opportunity to influence prices and therefore cannot exert any control. In fact, there are only a very few people and institutions who control the markets through high-volume trading. Even stock exchange gurus can influence the market only in the short term with their opinions. This is possible only in small markets, confirmed frequently and impressively by the recommendations of stock exchange gurus in the Neue Markt, even though the resulting exaggerated prices are always quickly corrected.

Even large injections of capital are frequently not sufficient to steer markets in the desired direction. Central banks in many countries have found this to their cost, when massive interventions have not been able to prevent the devaluation of a currency in the end. Take Nick Leeson, who discovered this himself when he brought the Barings Bank to bankruptcy in 1995. In general, most market participants are probably aware that they cannot influence prices. Consequently, they are not under the impression that they can control the market in any form.

Control through prediction
Individuals can take things into account and organize their actions in such a way that an event will turn out as favorably as possible if events can be predicted to a certain degree (Perkins 1968, Thompson 1981). Although the event cannot be influenced directly, people's own future situations can at least be shaped around this event.

Take, for instance, the manager of a company quoted on the stock exchange, who is aware of the turnover and profit his company makes. The manager could probably predict future prices for his company's shares more or less correctly, based on his insider knowledge, and could enter into transactions based on this information, i.e. he would have total control of his capital. Apart from exceptional cases such as this (which would, by the way, have serious legal repercussions for the manager), most investors will not be able to predict future price developments.

It is even more surprising that only very few investors know the limit of the extent to which prices can be predicted. An entire army of economic and technically oriented analysts are convinced they control the market on the basis of their own forecasts: predictions invoke the sense of being able to control the market. And they believe that the more logically they have been compiled, the more probable that they will come true. This phenomenon is called "control illusion", and is frequently seen on the stock exchange. We will return to this phenomenon later.

Control through awareness of the influence factors

The decision maker in the third variant is merely aware of the factors that govern a particular event, without him having any influence on its occurrence or outcome in any way. This knowledge still enables him to judge his own situation, and therefore lessens the feeling of helplessness. He may even be able to get the best out of the situation for his own purposes. Hedging one's risks, for example, only makes sense if the cause of the risk is known. For instance, if an investor has purchased Russian oil shares and wants to insure the risks associated with this, then he must know all the actual factors that influence the risk. These include, for example, exchange rates, volatile oil prices, credit-worthiness and political instability.

This control variant applies to a wide spectrum of decision-making situations, which nevertheless differ in the extent to which the control (or control deficit) is experienced. A decision maker considers a situation more or less controllable when he feels that he is fully informed and competent, so that he is confident he can reliably calculate the probability of an event occurring. An example would be the toss of a coin, where heads (50 per cent probability) would mean a gain of $110 and tails (also 50 per cent probability) would produce a loss of $100. Everything needed for a decision is known, so the risk can be calculated exactly and therefore controlled.

It is even more favorable if it is known that the decision-making situation will be repeated in future. Imagine, for instance, that the coin will be tossed 100 times. If you can calculate probability, you will see that the expected value of the game will be almost certainly achieved by tossing the coin a large number of times, based on the law of high numbers. Accordingly, a participant in the game will almost certainly have won a sum of approximately $500 when the coin has been tossed 100 times.[5] A similarly high number of games will probably still give rise to a decision to play, even if the amount of money that can be won is reduced to $101. The decision maker has the situation almost completely under control; this does not apply to the same extent to the one-shot situation, in which the coin is tossed once only (Samuelson 1963, Benartzi and Thaler 1995).

Such situations, characterized by full information and clearly indicated and reliable probability, are not typical for the financial markets. The actor is usually aware that he has only partial information in relation to his possible investment, and he can estimate probability only vaguely, if at all. Nevertheless, should he be asked to indicate probability precisely, then the quantification will be surrounded by ambiguity, i.e. he cannot be sure about the probability he has indicated.

For instance, a renowned analyst, who has extensively researched the current interest situation, predicts that interest rates will rise with a probability of 60 per cent, and a friend states that instinct tells him that interest rates might rise, perhaps with a probability of 60 per cent. Both statements would seem identical, but they differ in their reliability. The friend's statement is much less certain than that of the analyst.

As well as third-party statements, one's own estimation of probability can also be surrounded by ambiguity. For example, there are 50 red and 50 black balls in a barrel; a second container is also filled with 100 red and black balls, but in this case it is not known how many balls there are of each color. Participants select a barrel from which to remove a ball. They will receive $100 if the

---

[5] The total gain of $500 results when winning $10 ($110 win − $100 loss) in 100 games with a probability of 50 per cent (= $10 × 0.5 × 100).

ball is red, and nothing if the ball is black. Which container would you choose? Like most people, you would probably choose the first barrel, as the odds are known in this case (50 per cent). The indication of probability for winning in the case of the second barrel is full of ambiguity.

Investors may get into situations with high ambiguity, in particular when they enter markets that are new to them. Take an investor, for instance, who has so far traded only in German blue-chip shares and who also knows all relevant factors; he considers himself very competent and imagines that he can control the situation to some extent. How will the investor feel when he invests in Asian stocks? He knows few of the relevant factors, and his probability estimations are full of ambiguity. The investor will feel rather incompetent, even helpless; we should therefore not assume that he imagines he can even remotely control the situation. Most investors prefer to avoid such uncontrollable situations, as numerous empirical studies confirm. They prefer to invest in their own country, which they are familiar with, rather than abroad. This effect is known as "home asset preference effect" or "domestic bias" (Folkerts-Landau and Ito 1995, French and Poterba 1991).

Retrospective explanation of events

The fourth and weak control variant occurs when an event is explained retrospectively, i.e. after it has occurred. The main purpose is to arrive at knowledge about future similar situations, based on the explanation of events that have already occurred (Thompson 1981, Osnabrügge et al. 1998). Explaining an event primarily means to analyze its causes, and controlling the causes would enable one to control similar situations in future. The phenomenon of rape victims blaming themselves for the crime could be explained thus (Medea and Thompson 1974). The victim who blames herself may tell herself that it depends on her own behavior whether she will be attacked again, and that she could minimize the risk of being raped again and thus be in control. This strategy allows victims to anchor the locus of control in themselves, instead of feeling at the mercy of others in respect of the risk of a further attack and potential rape. This supposed control helps to overcome the experience psychologically.

The fourth control variant plays a role in the financial markets insofar as knowing the cause and effect in the markets can be extremely useful for subsequent investments. For instance, a person who has just lost a lot of money in a stock exchange crash will swear to do their utmost so that future risks are known well in advance and losses are avoided. The investor will begin to look for explanations for the crash. The danger is that the investor will reach conclusions prematurely, which need not necessarily be correct, in order to meet his urgent need for control. He will, for instance, soon recognize that this crash occurred in October, just like a number of previous crashes. He will decide that next year he will sell his shares in September to avoid another disaster. The myth of October as a "crash month" is thus created. The investor may well overlook the fact that the fall in prices was caused not because it was October, but occurred for a completely different reason, such as a currency crisis, which coincidentally occurred in October.

Control by playing down negative results
The fifth and weakest control variant refers to the ability to play down possible negative results of one's actions. This type of control is used by individuals who very quickly forget a painful event, or who can consistently steer their thoughts towards its (few) positive aspects (Thompson 1981). At the same time, they succeed in explaining away the blow fate has dealt them as part of a higher-level plan: "Now I know why that happened and what I can do about it next time."

Losses are therefore often played down as if they are the price to pay for learning. People tell themselves that they might have had to pay even more for this knowledge in a seminar, so they are still quids in. Characteristic for this control variant is that it ultimately leads to greater satisfaction via a change in perception of, or even attitude to, a situation. Unfortunately, there is no change in the real circumstances.

Control factors

Characteristic of investor behavior in the financial markets are the three control variants where causes, influences and factors in a particular situation are actively sought out in order to be in a better position to deal with similar occurrences in the future. Three factors are particularly important. Firstly, the size and the particular sign (plus or minus) of the sums that are the subject of the decision. Secondly, the uncertainty about the probability with which the desired or feared consequences of a decision will occur (ambiguity), as well as the competence of the decision maker. Thirdly, the question as to whether the results of several decisions were perceived individually or as a whole.

Size and signs of the sums involved

The initial factor that influences a decision is the size of the sum of money; whether we are dealing with a profit or a loss also plays a large role, of course. In the case of extremely low sums, there is little feeling of being at the mercy of something. The risk here is more in the nature of a gamble.[6] In contrast, large, and in particular negative (losses), amounts may well affect the life of the decision maker to a considerable degree. Take a possible case of liability, which can result in high payments if you are not insured, causing a considerable reduction in wealth over a lifetime. You do not want to get into such an uncertain situation, so that a strong desire for control is created, which can only be met by purchasing insurance. A parallel case is that of an exporter with large open-dollar positions, who will sleep better if the risk of an unfavorable price movement is covered by a futures contract or forward option.

An investor who has so far invested his money only in Europe might consider purchasing Russian stocks if it involves only a small amount of money. This investment would represent a gamble in the eyes of the investor; there would be no question of risking additional money.

Competence and ambiguity

Whether our investor invests in Russian stock or not also depends on his knowledge or competence. If he knows the main determining factors, and he is able to estimate probability without

---

[6]   Thaler and Johnson (1990) showed that small sums can lead to the "house money effect". People who have already won a certain amount of money in a casino will stake the money won (and therefore act as risk takers) when only part of it is at stake. They will, however, act risk-averse if the possible loss is larger than the amount previously won. Thaler and Johnson call this the "break-even effect".

ambiguity, which is therefore extremely reliable, then he will believe himself to be in control. But if the investor is competent only to a limited extent, and can only give a vague probability percentage, then the sense of not being in control of the situation becomes stronger (Heath and Tversky 1991, Keppe 1997). This control deficit is felt by most people as painful, so they prefer to avoid uncontrollable situations (ambiguity aversion). Only if the invested sum is small, and it is therefore possible to keep track of the risk of losing the money, will some people invest anyway. The higher the sum to be invested, the greater the sense of control deficit based on a lack of competence.

Individual evaluation or total evaluation of the result of actions
This important determining factor comes into play when a risky situation is repeated. Tossing a coin, for instance, shows that the risk is balanced when the number of individual games increases, so that the control deficit is reduced. Whether the results of the games in the series are considered individually or in total is paramount. If a decision maker posts the results of all the games to a single mental account (integration), then his control deficit in the case of a large number of games is less than in the case of a decision maker who plays only once, or who judges each gamble individually (segregation).

In the case of financial markets, this means that those investors who review their performances only after long intervals perceive the smallest control deficit. Investors who are exposed to the large daily price fluctuations, and check daily whether their shares have gained or lost, will perceive the risks as much larger and will soon experience the feeling that they are at the mercy of the markets. The behavior of investors who closely follow price movements was compared with that of investors who think in a long-term manner (Benartzi and Thaler 1995). It was shown that investors in the first group acted much more risk-averse and on the whole achieved worse results.

Mental accounts can be isolated not only over time, but also in respect of content. Refer back to the example in Chapter 3, in which shares (bathing costumes and rainwear) with contrasting risks were analyzed. It became clear that a decision maker who leans heavily on mental accounting will reject both investments on the basis of the high control deficit in each case. On the other hand, a decision maker who runs a joint account for both investments will recognize that the risks are balanced and will perceive only a minimal control deficit in his total position after the purchase of the shares.

Consequences of the need for control

The strategy to simply block out certain information in order to avoid cognitive dissonance is called "selective perception". This is also said to help reduce dissonance. Similarly, control illusion is said to reduce the control deficit at least apparently; it therefore satisfies the need for control. People only imagine they are master of the situation – in reality they usually do not control the situation by any means (Langner 1975).

Selective decision making describes the behavior whereby people in particular situations decide in a way such that dissonance is reduced. The sunk cost effect is an important example, according to which people try to move loss projects associated with dissonance into the profit zone by means of (irrational) decisions. The counterpart to the need for control consists of the phenomenon of loss of control, which similarly gives rise to irrational decision-making patterns (e.g. panic response).

A third consequence of the need to be free from dissonance was shown to be loss or regret aversion, an effect that gives rise to possible dissonance, even before a decision is made, through the anticipation of possible dissonance. People overvalue losses disproportionally, as these invoke dissonance. Similarly, the concept of risk aversion can be traced to the perception of a possible control deficit: people act in a risk-averse way because they experience a painful need for control that has not yet been met. Table 5-1 summarizes the similarity between the consequences from both motives.

Illusion of control
The illusion of control is when a person believes that they are master of a situation, when in reality they are not. The term "overconfidence" is used when the illusion of control is related to

Table 5-1   Similarity between the consequences of the need to be free of dissonance and the need for control

	Need to be free from dissonance	Need for control
Meeting the need through perception of a situation	Selective perception	Control illusion
Meeting the need through a particular decision	Selective decision making	Phenomenon of loss of control
Perception of a possible deficit	Loss and regret of aversion	Risk aversion

predictability of events (Lichtenstein et al. 1982). People tend to have a disproportionally great confidence in their own ability (in this case their own forecasts), a source of errors that systematically distorts perception. In practice, this leads, for example, to analysts often compiling forecast bands that are too narrow. The greater the confidence a person has in themselves, the more risk there is of overconfidence.[7] This applies, in particular, to areas where people are not well-informed – self-confidence usually bears no relation to their knowledge. This behavior also arises from the need for control, and the fact that people imagine they have mastered a subject, when they merely have some superficial knowledge of it. A surprising aspect is the relationship between overconfidence and competence. March and Shapira (1987) showed that managers overestimate the probability of success in particular when they think of themselves experts.

Control illusion is an extremely important phenomenon in relation to the financial markets. Two sides meet in the case of a transaction. One side (the buyer) predicts rising future prices, and the other (the seller) assumes falling prices. The markets thrive on the different forecasts by the actors and the actors' belief in these forecasts. Few transactions would be concluded without a conviction of control (Maas and Weibler 1990b). De Bondt and Thaler (1995) said: "Overconfidence explains why portfolio managers trade so much, why pension funds hire active equity managers, and why even financial economists often hold actively managed portfolios – they all think they can pick winners." Control illusion

---

[7]   Note that there is no linear relationship between self-confidence and overconfidence.

becomes problematic the moment it causes exposures to become too large and associated risks to be underestimated. Market participants, for example, who have been lucky more than once in a row will start to overestimate their capabilities, stake everything out of pure greed, and therefore run risks from which they would have shrunk if the illusion of control had not made them blind in respect of a realistic consideration of the situation.

Control illusion can, however, be traced back to aspects other than the desire to satisfy the need for control. Most people assume that the more control they have, the sooner they will be able to influence matters positively for themselves. This schema is easily reversed as part of the conditional probability fallacy. Once someone succeeds several times in succession, he will be convinced that things are under his control. Representativity therefore supports the illusion of control (Abramson and Alloy 1980).

The phenomenon of control illusion can also be derived from attribution theory. An important part of this theory is the "self-esteem serving attribution": if people succeed, then they believe this to be due solely to personal skills; if something goes wrong, then others, or adverse circumstances, are to blame. Market participants succeeding in the financial markets will take all the credit themselves. They will be under a strong illusion of control after a fairly long series of successes: they seem to succeed in everything. If they are not successful, then investors remind themselves (and others) that success on the stock exchange always depends on luck. That time they have been unlucky. Self-esteem serving attribution therefore also contributes to the creation of control illusion.

The phenomenon of "learned carelessness" is linked closely to control illusion. With this phenomenon, an actor has had a series of successful investments and no longer knows what it feels like to lose. He is therefore prepared to run ever larger risks (Frey and Schulz-Hardt 1996, Schulz-Hardt et al. 1996). Nick Leeson, for instance, was so successful for a relatively long period that he was called the "man with the golden touch" by his colleagues in Singapore. He seemed to be able to produce large profits for the Barings Bank with hardly any effort. The results of his increasing carelessness, growing into foolishness and megalomania, are well-known.

Availability also comes into the equation here, which ultimately states that the importance of events for the evaluation of a situation decreases as availability of these events decreases. The more time has passed since losses were made, or the less visible or noticeable a loss stored in the memory, the less risk plays a role in the evaluation of exposures and the greater and more risky the deals become. Learned carelessness therefore leads to the same consequences as control illusion.

"Hindsight bias" is the tendency on the part of many people to overestimate what they knew or suspected about the outcome of an event before it took place (Fischhoff 1975): "I knew it!" This effect is seen when a trader muses, after he has missed the chance to enter a long position against a rising dollar price, "I knew that the dollar was on the up. Why didn't I buy then?" He probably did not *know* at all. Nobody knows exactly whether a price will rise or fall. In retrospect, however, many people seem to remember that they had a feeling that it would be so. The same investor would probably have said that he was in a bearish mood all along if the dollar price had fallen.

The link with control illusion lies in the fact that people don't want to admit to themselves that they have very little control over a particular situation. They therefore like to imagine that they actually knew at the time what would happen. It is surprising how many investors report after a crash that they had seen it coming, that they could have known the outcome all along, and that the price was much too high. The question remains, why did these investors not sell their shares in order to avoid large losses? Hindsight bias can therefore also be interpreted as retrospective control illusion.

Loss of control phenomena

Many of the empirical studies relating to the importance of the need for control concern themselves mainly with loss of control. This occurs when someone initially assumes to control a particular event or a situation, or at least to be able to influence it strongly, and later has to admit that he cannot exercise this control at all (for example, as a result of control illusion). This admission can lead to serious frustration, uncertainty, or even fear and panic (Miller and Norman 1979, Sauer and Müller 1980). People with a strong need to control suffer when experiencing loss of control (Fazio et al. 1981).

There are two possible responses to a loss of control. First, one can call on someone who still seems to be master of the situation.[8] This could be a well-known analyst or a stock exchange guru whose forecasts have always, or frequently, been right in the past. As we explained in the section on representativity, this does not necessarily mean anything. Nevertheless, the investor feels less at the mercy of market events if he follows the advice of an analyst.

This was proven to be the case on the American Stock Exchange (Schachter et al. 1986). The study investigated how reading the *Wall Street Journal* column "Read on the street" affected investor behavior. In this column, well-known stock exchange experts stated their opinions on present and future developments in the financial markets. These opinions had only a small effect on investor behavior at a time when share prices rose, but the effect was significantly greater in times of falling prices, as most investors encountered problems (loss of control).

Another way is to seek out groups of people with similar opinions, e.g. investment clubs. The investor is no longer alone, as comparing opinions in the group creates an illusion of validity, which simultaneously restores the feeling of control: "After all, this many people cannot be wrong."

If investors are unable to regain control, then the second response variant kicks in. In this case, general and quickly available response patterns are activated, which means that the person becomes stressed. People under stress either become angry and attack, or they retreat.

Market participants in the financial markets experience loss of control when, believing themselves to be firmly in control of the market after a long period of continuous profit, and having entered into large exposures, suddenly everything goes against them. The feeling of certain success turns out to be an illusion of control. In addition, the actors may not even be able to explain this surprising course of events retrospectively or they amass contradictions in their information (Maas and Weibler 1990b). Many give a "We'll show them!" response in order to save the exposure and to regain the illusory control. A share that has fallen in value is then purchased again in order to reduce the purchase price. Retreat often follows only when it becomes clear that these shares will not

[8]   Rothbaum et al. (1982) speak of "substitute control".

lead to the desired result. Such a situation becomes particularly dangerous when many market participants simultaneously display such behavior and all want to escape through the same door.

Evaluation of a control deficit: risk aversion
Would you describe yourself as risk-averse or as a risk taker? Most people will say that they cannot give a general answer to this question. There are people who invest their money in very risky investments and projects, but who would not dream of taking part in dangerous sports, such as parachuting. Individual willingness to accept risk would seem to depend essentially on the situation or, to be more precise, on the control deficit in each situation. If we believe that it is possible to master or even to control the risk, then the behavior is not so much risk-averse but rather that of a risk taker. On the other hand, if we suspect a control deficit, then the behavior becomes risk-averse and we will avoid situations that are felt to be threatening (von Nitzsch and Friedrich 1999). This explains why a risk-taking investor need not necessarily be an enthusiastic parachutist or bungee jumper.

So, if risk aversion results from a control deficit, then the determining factors for the extent of risk aversion arise at the same time as the determining factors for a control deficit. This implies the following:

- Risk aversion increases with an increase in the amounts of money at risk following a decision, and is greater in the case of negative sums than in the case of positive sums.
- Risk aversion increases as competence decreases or if the probability that an event will occur cannot be clearly predicted.
- Risk aversion increases with the tendency to post the results of a decision to separate mental accounts.

It follows that nobody has a fixed attitude to risk in respect of everything, but that the attitude to risk can vary considerably, depending on the decision-making situation.[9]

A control deficit need not necessarily always lead to risk aversion. There are also situations where people experience loss of

---

[9] In particular, risk aversion that is reduced as the capital increases (e.g. see Oehler 1998) can also be explained by the fact that people experience a control deficit as less painful when their capital is growing.

control positively. This is the case, for instance, when the chance of a win is minimal, but the risk of a threatened loss is estimated as very great. In such a situation, people do not reject ambiguous probability (see also Camerer and Weber 1992), but instead deliberately choose these from a number of possibilities in the hope that the almost impossible win will occur and the almost certain loss can perhaps yet be averted. This "logic" is used by participants in national lotteries. People prefer to remain pleasurably uncertain, leaving them with a shimmer of hope for the main prize. Who likes to be told how stupid they have been buying yet another lottery ticket and how improbable the desired win actually is?

In addition, people need a number of stimuli so as not to fall into apathy and mindlessness. Locking someone into a totally dark and quiet room entirely devoid of stimuli is the worst punishment imaginable. Even a certain risk can be experienced as stimulating, including the slight thrills that keep people going in casinos, on race tracks or up steep mountain sides (Brengelmann 1991), which might explain the phenomenon of risk taking.

IS RISK AVERSION RATIONAL?
DOES MONEY BRING HAPPINESS?

We stated earlier that a rational decision is characterized by the fact that only its consequences are weighed up. We saw that in relation to the sunk cost effect, it is not rational to take into account costs incurred in the past, as this may lead to decisions that are less than optimal. The fact that one would have mainly hoped for a reduction in dissonance would have been paramount.

Interesting, far-reaching answers for the question, "What risk attitudes are rational?", arise if we rate the need for consonance at the same level as the control motive. We could argue that it is not rational to behave risk-averse, analogous to the irrationality of the sunk cost effect. Ultimately, risk aversion is invoked by an unmet need for control, just like aversion in respect of dissonance is a response to the need to be free of dissonance.

The following example shows that there is some sense in attributing a degree of reason to the disposition effect. Take an investor with a stock position that now makes a loss. The investor should dispose of his position on the basis of rationality if he can invest the money and get better returns elsewhere. This decision would be sensible from a financial point of view but it would be at the cost of satisfaction and the well-being of the investor: first he must admit that he made a wrong decision in the past; second, this action would destroy any change of the investment producing any profit after all. Should the investor decline to realize his loss, and instead hold on to the shares until they produce a profit, then he will ultimately have a successful investment, even though it has taken some time. This will prevent him from investing in other, more lucrative transactions, but it would keep him happy.

We deliberately leave unanswered the question as to whether it is rational (economically and overall) to buy satisfaction through the rejection of a more profitable investment. Ultimately, we are dealing with the question as to whether money or the fulfillment of other needs (e.g. the need for control and freedom of dissonance) brings happiness. There is no doubt, however, that fulfillment of these needs must be bought at a price. The quest for fulfillment of the need for control is linked to the payment of a risk premium; to reduce dissonance, one must be prepared to make decisions that are not always optimal.

Chapter 6

Everyone is different

Three types of market participant

Having seen that market participants do not always act rationally in everyday trading situations, even if they intend to, you will want to know how you can use this knowledge. You will also want to know how to avoid the mistakes and errors discussed. You may well have recognized yourself in one of the scenarios, or you may argue that cognitive dissonance and control illusion are nothing new. Self-knowledge alone, however, is not sufficient to change behavior in the markets and to achieve greater profits.

Behavioral finance on the stock exchange and in trading firms is not "soft psychology". We are dealing not with unimportant incidental facts but with repeated patterns of behavior and behavioral outcomes that sometimes even culminate in large speculative bubbles, which many analysts can respond to only by shaking their heads with lack of understanding. What they see appears to them to be completely irrational. Holding out against irrationality, however, could be extremely expensive, both in psychological energy and in terms of money.

Anyone with a better understanding of irrationality in the markets, having read this book, and who is also willing to cast a critical and careful eye on his own day-to-day trading in the markets, is already a winner. You are likely to see increased profits in the financial markets, as well as gains in everyday life. For the market is nothing but a mirror reflecting human actions and responses. Markets in which goods, services, ideas etc. are exchanged may spring up quickly at places where people meet. Anyone who knows anything about the psychologically induced effects on participants in these markets will increasingly be able to sell their goods at a higher price, or buy cheaper, given a modicum of luck.

We have compiled a system to prevent the route to successful trading from being applied piecemeal. At first glance, the system may seem simple, but it is not so easy to implement in real life. One's own mind often sabotages the discipline required. People tend to choose the road of least resistance at the decisive moment. A departure from the norm, from what they have always done, or from the way problems used to be resolved in the past suddenly seems unbearable: "I would like to, but I can't." This "but" causes them to remain ensnared in their own lack of discipline; if they are lucky, they may not be punished by failure.

There is no cure-all for human weakness in the markets. Readers may have found some examples to be more relevant than others. Some may have judged the section on control more important, while others may relate more to the findings regarding cognitive dissonance. Some readers may have concluded that a review of everyday processes and methods is called for. Many people will not know where to start, having the impression that everything they have read applies to them. It therefore makes sense to divide market participants into different types or categories. We have chosen a system in which people can recognize themselves quickly, so they can take measures to combat the weaknesses inherent in the type that applies to them.

Character traits determine at which stage of a transaction they need to take particular care and which false conclusions they should guard against. As this is based mostly on the structure of the human brain, we refer to the theory of the "triune brain", devised by the neurophysiologist Paul D. MacLean (MacLean 1977,

MacLean 1978, MacLean 1983, MacLean 1985, MacLean 1990, MacLean 1993), idealized somewhat in order to explain our theory of types. We will demonstrate at a later stage that these types fit certain groups of market participants particularly well.[1] Each type, and therefore each group, of market participants, has a characteristic psychological profile that is particularly susceptible to certain weaknesses in respect of rationality. Before we study these associations in greater detail, let us discuss the triune brain.

THE TRIUNE BRAIN

Neurophysiologist Paul D. MacLean, head of the laboratory for brain development and behavior at the National Institute of Health in Maryland, USA, claims that the human brain consists of three independent brains, functionally speaking (MacLean 1990), that have developed over the course of evolution. Each has a different structure and chemical composition. Each individual brain works independently of the others, although their functions partly overlap. Although inadequate coordination between the three separate brains can cause many problems, their structures must not be viewed in isolation: the three systems are integrated into a single brain, the "triune brain".

The oldest of these three brains is the reptile brain (also called R-complex), which came into being about 500 million years ago (Holler 1996). Continued development gave rise to the second brain, the limbic system,[2] with the evolution of mammals 200 to 300 million years ago. The youngest brain evolved some 100,000 years ago (Vroon 1993); it characterizes mammals of the modern era, the human species in particular – the cerebral cortex, or the neocortex, which is responsible for thinking, learning, problem solving, language etc. (Figure 6-1).

Although we might expect that a newer brain would have

---

[1] The neurobiological basis from which MacLean has developed this theory will be ignored for our purposes.

[2] MacLean suggested this name for the limbic cortex and the parts of the brain stem to which it is connected in the first instance.

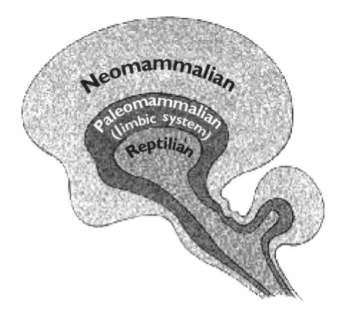

Figure 6-1   The triune brain, showing the reptile brain (Reptilian), limbic
system (Paleomammalian) and youngest brain (Neomammalian).
Source: MacLean (1990).

replaced a less developed brain in the course of evolution, this was
not the case. Instead, nature added the new brain to the already
existing one. According to MacLean, the human brain can be
compared with three biological computers, each possessing its own
"intelligence", memory, emotions and other functions. It is as if
the brain is driven by three different people, each with their own
characteristics.

MacLean suggested that the two older structures of the brain,
the R-complex and the limbic system, not only influence human
behavior but also cause many of the problems people face everyday. These structures are not able to communicate with the parts of
the brain that are responsible for language, but this does not mean
that they are less intelligent or "subconscious". Emissions from the
psyche have no material substance. They need to be "translated"
into behavior in order to be able to communicate them. As a result,
human behavior is divided into non-verbal and verbal behavior.

There are certainly similarities between non-verbal human actions and animal patterns of behavior. This is not surprising, as the human brain was built on to the animal brain during the course of evolution, and has certain parts in common with the animal brain.

MacLean did not think it appropriate to compare non-verbal human behavior with animal behavior, so he decided to use the Greek term *prosemantic* for any kind of non-verbal messages. This means " to signal", vocally, bodily or chemically.

Looking at the reptile brain, non-verbal behavior includes the selection and creation of a home, choosing and defending one's territory, hunting, herd instinct, and formation of social groups. Reptiles have an almost perfect memory for what their predecessors have experienced over the course of thousands of years, but they are probably not capable of learning from new situations. The corresponding human actions apply mainly to everyday routines, for which people tend to rely on tradition, including one's own rituals, copying previous processes, ceremonies that have been enacted over and over again, actions conditioned by superstition, and all kinds of errors.

Differences in behavior between reptiles and mammals (and birds) in the evolutionary process manifest themselves in three basic changes in development for which the limbic system is said to be responsible. The first point is feeding and rearing the young. Secondly, communication based on hearing and the voice arose to ensure contact between the female and her young, as well as encouraging play amongst the young, i.e. to encourage emotional behavior, required for self-preservation. Dorsch et al. (1994) have shown that the limbic system controls emotional behavior and thus the emotional framework of humans and animals. This includes emotions such as fear, panic, anger, love, ecstasy etc. (Holler 1996). The limbic system seems also to be the source of human value judgments: it decides whether something is considered right or wrong, and coordinates emotional behavior.

The neocortex is characterized primarily by its ability to learn and think. The latter could be considered a medium to organize, interpret and understand impulses from the non-verbal part of the brain (Joseph 1988). The neocortex focuses in the first place on the external world and seems to function as a problem solver and memory (MacLean 1983). The neocortex on its own could be compared with a "heartless computer" that makes only rational decisions. It can therefore help the two older parts of the brain to survive as human beings. There are, nevertheless, signs that it is difficult for the organism to make these decisions exclusively on a rational basis, as it constantly receives signals from its "heart", which prevents purely rational behavior.

Finally, nature ensures that the neocortex receives its information mostly from the senses through seeing, hearing and feeling. The neocortex is, however, often not capable of suppressing or regulating impulses from the limbic system.

MacLean has tested his theory of the brain with the aid of numerous studies and experiments on animals because he could not conduct such experiments on people. He was also able to examine people with different brain diseases, such as epilepsy. These findings ultimately led him to the conclusion that the three brains each produce a different mentality – instinct, emotions and reason – which are often in conflict with each other. Our brain is not a uniform entity, but a stack of three systems (Vroon 1993).

It is likely that individuals tend to use one element of the triune brain somewhat more intensively than the other two. This does not mean, of course, that someone who uses his reptile brain in preference to the others behaves like an animal. Rather, we must assume that the tendency to prefer one of the three mentalities – instinct, emotions or reason (we could also say acting, feeling or thinking) – basically shapes a person's character. We will use the term "gut people" for those who make instinctive decisions, "heart people" for those who act on emotions, and "head people" for those who indicate a strong preference for reason.

Not every individual can be categorized clearly as one of these types, as although people may use one part of the brain in preference, they also use the other two components to a smaller extent. Ultimately, we are dealing with a blend of types, although an emphasis on one of the three characteristics can be seen in everyone.

The main point is that there is a link between the three character types – head, heart and gut – and the susceptibility for the cognitive errors and failures described in Chapters 3–5. It is sensible to limit these to the five basic instances of rationality described below.

PSYCHOGRAM OF AN INVESTOR: THE FIVE MAIN INSTANCES INVOLVING RATIONALITY

Chapters 3–5 contain a large number of possible weaknesses in decision-making behavior by market participants. Chapter 3 discussed the rules of thumb that people use to reduce complexity in decision-making situations and to arrive quickly at a judgment. We showed in detail how systematic errors creep in and what the consequences are.

We then discussed a particular feature of the evaluation process in Chapter 4: generally, people evaluate relatively rather than absolutely. There is a reference point for each evaluation, which leads to a distinction between relative gains and relative losses. This reference point is often represented by the purchase price as far as market participants are concerned. This is accompanied by systematic departures from rational behavior because actors take too much risk below the purchase price, and are overcautious in the profit zone.

Chapter 5 described the negative effects certain motives or emotions can have on rationality. On the one hand, market participants strive to be free of dissonance. They want always to make the right decisions and do something (often irrational) in order to make themselves and others believe that they are successful. They will, for instance, only take note of information that puts their (possibly bad) decisions in a good light; they only absorb new information selectively. They do not clear their loss-making exposures as this would confirm their bad decisions. On the other hand, market participants have a strong need for control, and they hate being at the mercy of a situation. This leads to two problems. Firstly, most participants overestimate their own capabilities to anticipate price developments, which may lead to very risky decisions, occasionally resulting in large losses. Secondly, the need for control is ultimately responsible for the fact that market participants, insofar as they think they are losing control, become stressed, fearful or panicky, and will therefore no longer act rationally.

Considering the irrational behavior patterns, it is possible to identify five aspects as the main instances of rationality.

Use of heuristics: "premature acting"

This market participant allows himself only a short time to consider the current situation and refers to comparatively little information. His problem is that the information easily available to him determines his judgment, and therefore his exposures, to a disproportionately large extent. This often leads to wrong judgments and non-optimum decisions. He also thinks in certain patterns or stereotypes. He easily falls victim to certain wrong conclusions and errors. For instance, he will see connections merely because they fit into a schema, even if they do not really exist.

Relative evaluation: "identifies too much with the purchase price"

This actor typically keeps an individual account in his head for each exposure. He strongly identifies with the purchase price and would like to close each of his accounts in profit. He will tend towards risk taking in respect of exposures that are doomed, i.e. he will let losses run. He likes to increase his position in the case of a more favorable price, lowering the purchase price. At the same time, he is risk-averse in the case of exposures that are doing well, and he tends therefore to take his profits too early.

Striving to be free of dissonance: "committed to decisions"

This market participant will only admit with difficulty that he must have made a mistake with a particular transaction. He formally stands by his decision and is looking for opportunities to get out of a loss situation. His problem is that he needs to liquidate his loss-making exposure at the purchase price or higher, even if this no longer makes sense, or would seem to be impossible. He therefore tends to overestimate the chances of a profit on shares that have fallen steeply in value, merely so as not to have to admit to himself or others that he has made a mistake. He will only take note of information that suits his purpose, while he largely plays down, or even ignores, news that he finds unpalatable.

Control illusion: "overestimating control opportunities"

These people tend to overestimate their capability to forecast prices, in particular after a successful transaction. They believe themselves to be master of the situation and therefore take excessive risks. As a result, they risk holding on to their forecasts or investment decisions for too long. This type of actor has usually invested a lot of money in a few stocks, and is fully convinced that they will lead to a profit. This investor often trades in a single market segment. His objective is to look good in public and to become rich as quickly as possible.

Loss of control phenomena: "fear of non-controllable exposures"

This actor has an urgent need to control the risk inherent in his exposure. He prefers to be well-informed, and becomes stressed when he has to admit that he cannot control the situation. He feels hopelessly at the mercy of things in case of violent price fluctuations. Losses make him nervous and cause him to act impulsively. This actor therefore avoids such situations, and at the same time possibly misses many lucrative investments.

A survey of more than 30,000 market participants based on the PsychoTrainer[3] shows that there are hardly any market participants who do not admit to one or more of these errors. Many are at

---

[3] The PsychoTrainer, developed by the authors of this book, is freely available on the Börse Online homepage (**www.boerse-online.de**).

risk of only one or two of the instances described, but others need to be extremely careful as they are susceptible to all rationality instances.

On this basis, each market participant can be summed up clearly with the aid of a "susceptibility profile", which lists the instances to which each person is particularly susceptible. Figure 6-2 shows an example of such a profile. The size of the bars (the percentages) indicates the rationality instances for which the test person must be on his guard. The illustration shows the profile of a market participant who identifies strongly with purchase prices and at the same time sticks with his own decisions. He does not act prematurely, nor does he overestimate his chances of control. His fear of uncontrollable exposures is minimal.

This investor might come up against the disposition effect in particular, i.e. he will realize profits too soon and will leave losses to run. At the same time, he will only collect information that supports his exposure, which may lead to additional problems.

The profile illustrated is only an example, however. A different market participant might, for instance, generally decide on the basis of a rule of thumb and also identify strongly with the purchase price. Someone else may have collected comprehensive information and in addition care little about the purchase price, but he may be rather too much convinced of the quality of his forecasts.

This begs the question, is it possible to develop a "fitting" susceptibility profile for the three types (gut, heart and head people)? It could well be that there are particular groups, perhaps even occupational groups, amongst market participants who could be assigned a type or a fitting susceptibility profile.

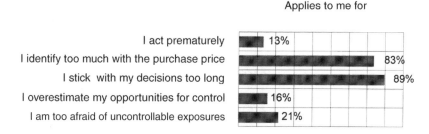

Figure 6-2 Suceptibility profile.

THREE TYPES OF MARKET PARTICIPANT

It would seem a good idea to start by applying the theory of types developed above to the financial markets. This can be done without difficulty, as market participants are, after all, human, i.e. individuals with triune brains. Even so, not every market participant will fit into this structure. The human character simply has too many layers and aspects. Nevertheless, we would expect that most readers identify with one type more than any other. People may also recognize that they are a blend, for instance between gut and head.

Acting on gut feeling: the intuitive type

Human behavior still has remnants of instinctive behavior patterns stored in the reptile brain, even after millions of years. These include the need to build a "nest", which in today's terms can be read as owning a piece of land and defending it. The oldest part of the brain – the dominant part for gut people – is, in the main, responsible for daily routines. These include the continuously repeated rituals of which people are normally not even aware, such as getting up in the morning, washing, making coffee, and eating breakfast. These are "programs" that often do not change at all during the course of a lifetime.

Life for gut people consists of such routines and patterns of behavior that are easily available. It only becomes problematic when the programs are disturbed. Imagine that you have been woken very early in the morning by a knock at the door. Immediately, you will be in a state of alarm, which may be expressed as fear ("I hope nothing has happened"), anger ("Who dares to call at this time?") or even paralysis (you don't respond at all).

These routines correspond to profitable exposures in the financial markets. Life's task and occupational objective in the case of gut people certainly does not consist of making losses; on the contrary, they are "programmed" for profit. They rely on the positive characteristics of their reptile brain, have a feeling for profitable transactions and favorable situations, and act intuitively.

Typical market participant circles for gut people

Gut people are generally found where intuitive decisions are required, i.e. in an environment that requires intensive trading, in particular within a short timeframe. Gut people do not analyze situations carefully even when they have sufficient time at their disposal. Why should they? They are much better at making decisions based on gut feeling. We suspect that gut people can be found particularly amongst groups of market participants whose actions cover a short-term timeframe.

This group includes day traders. Conditions for these actors have improved considerably of late. Intraday trading is no longer anything unusual. The market in online brokerage is lively and cheap, and there are constantly new developments. Day traders usually have no time to analyze information, despite the comparatively plentiful supply of information available via the Internet. For instance, they respond immediately to an ad hoc report or rumor, so as to be amongst the first. They define themselves though trading; their motto is: "I trade, therefore I am."

Intuitive market participants also include traders, for instance in currencies, and brokers. Their main activity consists of pricing (setting market prices) and the immediate clearing of positions offered. Even if they are forced to hold on to these exposures, this is usually for only a few hours and is normally limited to one or two days. Normally only small price fluctuations will be exploited, and often the requirement is for particularly quick action. This enables the trader to exploit the spread advantage, i.e. the difference between the purchase and selling price, or the cash price and the asking price of the security or the currency. The spread advantage can, however, be exploited only fully in quiet markets – this is not always possible in volatile and frantic conditions. Nowadays, traders being offered positions by a third party must respond very quickly in order to avoid a loss on liquidation.

In addition, there are traders who enter into exposures on behalf of their banks. These are the proprietary traders. They try to exploit large price developments with the aid of information and opinions. They often hang on to positions – if they have the discipline and tenacity – for a number of weeks and can therefore not really be classed within this group. Mostly this group acts within a timeframe of days, and often only hours. Proprietary traders are, by nature, solitary actors. Although they collect a great deal of information and data, which they exchange with other market participants, the decision on the composition and clearing of an exposure will be entirely their responsibility.

The short-term oriented trader is also under pressure of having to make a profit, as his performance can be measured at any time. Normally, the process of making a profit takes place at least once a day. Often, it is not only their own profits that are important. Colleagues' results are also compared. This comparison not only forms the basis for an assessment for later remuneration in the form of a bonus, but is also a question of honor, as this determines the current social status in the group. Imagine the situation of a trader who reports a loss three days running, while the other contestants announce profitable results. Although for some this could be a stimulus to perform better, for others this means increased pressure to perform, accompanied by psychological symptoms, such as fear of failure and frustration. The same applies to the private investor, except that there is normally no competitive pressure from third parties (apart from acquaintances or friends whom he envies) – the only pressure he feels is from his own purse.

Often, increased frequency of trading and higher psychological pressure go together. Either the trader wants to make up for lost ground and wishes to rescue his reputation, or he is driven by the motive of envy of the profit made by others. Experience shows us that the actor does not necessarily make more profit when the frequency of trading is increased; rather, he responds to each new piece of information and to every price development, however small.

Susceptibility profile of the intuitive market participant
As the intuitive actor spends very little time on his decisions, he must make use of the advantages of subconscious routines. And because everything must be done quickly, he tends to simplify complex facts to a large extent. The gut person will resort to heuristics for this purpose, in order to be able to judge the situation in seconds, even though there is a danger that he is dealing with myths. He will not spend time on prolonged evaluations, and he refers to comparatively little information. Only those messages

that are easily and quickly available influence his judgments and therefore his commitments. He is an easy victim of his own selective observation. He could well miss unexpected pieces of information that need more time for processing than information that is easily available.

All heuristics described in this book could prove to be stumbling blocks for gut people. Errors occur in particular when several positions must be opened and closed quickly at the same time, as the amount of information required is usually too much and often too complex to be mastered within a short period of time. Losing time could, however, mean that the position is entered too late, as other market participants will possibly already have acted on the information. Opening and clearing positions is generally undertaken in a frantic and too rapid manner. The trading frequency could increase to such an extent that the minimal profit in the end does not even cover the transaction costs (trading spreads, commission etc.)

The most important information, which is also easiest to remember, for the gut type is the purchase price of his exposure. He evaluates each exposure individually, as the purchase price is usually the only thing he remembers. It is therefore not surprising that he will try to realize profits too early in the first instance, while he prefers to have nothing to do with losses – this type of person has hardly any ritualized behavior suitable for dealing with a loss. This is why most problems arise here, as the disposition effect is allowed to run its fatal course unabated. In addition, high susceptibility to the rationality instance, "identification with the purchase price", applies.

The gut person will try to respond to new events and developments with action. This applies to threats as well as rewards. His motives are of a purely material nature, i.e. he would like to hang on to what he has earned. Animal defense of territory has, in this case, developed into the behavior pattern of hanging on to what has been achieved. The gut person makes snap decisions. He strives only to do the usual in the situation: departures from the norm are outside his remit. This, in turn, leads to the fact that he won't put excessive store by his individual decisions. He would certainly prefer it if all his exposures would end in profit, but he knows that many successful tries by definition also include less successful attempts.

The gut person is not immune to letting losses run for too long, in particular as he usually finds it easy to justify his "normal" actions retrospectively. He shows great talent in releasing information and forecasts that justify his original actions retrospectively. This normally boils down to the fact that he can explain clearly why *he* is right when the market is behaving irrationally. There is therefore no reason to realize the loss suffered. We could suggest that there is a direct relationship between the size of the loss and the length of the justifying explanation. Gut people firmly believe that reason will, ultimately, prevail.

The gut person is convinced of his own capability. He thinks, "I am bound to do the right thing; after all, I can rely on my intuition." He is always ready to act by trading, and at the same time perceives some measure of control over the situation through his constant willingness to trade. Gut people believe firmly believe that they can save problematic situations by their own actions, or that they can quickly profit from favorable situations. They would, of course, prefer to permanently check the prices of shares, futures and currency that they trade, so as to achieve an even better performance. Many acquire an information system to connect them real time to the market, which turns them into screen junkies. Gut people can always depend on their behavior patterns. They are the market makers, and their actions count. Once they have concluded successfully several transactions in a row, they soon believe that they can achieve anything, i.e. they begin to overestimate their own capabilities and tend towards overconfidence. As a result, they risk having to chalk up considerable losses.

The maxim of the instinctively acting actor is, "Decide quickly, invest quickly and realize profits as quickly as possible." The routine is interrupted when the markets suddenly behave differently to what they expect. Developments and surprising innovations that appear illogical could have an effect on the gut person, similar to the surprising early-morning caller in the case of a person used to an unchanging routine. They invoke his anger, yet if the situation becomes unclear, he will wait and see. Aggression as an emotional expression is usually expressed verbally: he will swear loudly, as he must on no account show himself to be weak. Do not be surprised if you receive a rather curt reply to your question from a gut person in such a situation. Gut people get into

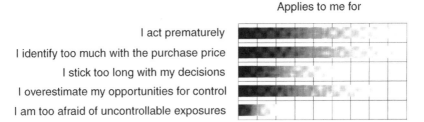

Figure 6-3   Typical susceptibility profile for an intuitive market participant.

panics very rarely; they tend to hang on to the belief that they are still in control of everything for a very long time.

Figure 6-3 summarizes this in a susceptibility profile. Hatching at the end of the bars means that only tendencies can be depicted in such a profile: exact manifestations depend on the individual. The main point is that the intuitively inclined actor must, in the first instance, pay careful attention to the rationality instances, "acting prematurely" and "identifying with the purchase price". He is particularly inclined to overestimate his opportunities for control following favorable outcomes of his exposures. At the same time, he sticks with his decisions, but this does not dominate his behavior. He is never afraid.

Wholeheartedly involved: the emotional type

The heart person is dominated by the limbic system. It was this part of the human brain that succeeded for the first time in communicating by hearing and the voice during the course of evolution. However, the markets are concerned not with rearing young ones, but with establishing and nurturing relationships between human beings. As the limbic system seems to be responsible for human value judgments, it is not surprising that this actor depends heavily on the way others evaluate his behavior.

As before, there is no agreement as to what emotions consist of and which emotions can be identified. Nevertheless, Elster (1999) has classified emotions to some extent.[4] Social emotions, such as

---

[4]   Jon Elster (1999) uses a seven-class system. We will mention only those emotions that are most relevant to market participants.

anger, hate, guilt, shame, admiration and affection, can be grouped together. Another group includes emotions that arise from uncertainty about future events, such as hope and fear, with which market participants are only too familiar. A third group includes emotions invoked by events that should (or should not) have occurred: regret, pleasant surprise and disappointment.

Market participants who are emotionally oriented will encounter problems particularly with the feelings of the second and third groups. They will try to protect the self and ego, so the psyche may survive unscathed. On the other hand, they thrive on positive vibrations and signals from other people. Their fundamental motive is to be loved, hence the term "heart people". They will typically try to reinforce positive feelings and suppress negative ones, showing themselves to be understanding and generous. However, they may also try to influence other people to their own advantage, for the motive of wanting to be loved often gives rise to strongly egotistical and grasping, if not manipulative, behavior.

The emotional market participant does not like to make trading decisions on his own – he would rather exchange opinions with others before taking action. He prefers to get together with a group of people who are like-minded.[5] The group as a basis for decision making is preferred by many heart people, as it is an instrument par excellence for reflecting the different opinions on the part of individuals, promoting well-being and confirmation. It means one is able to express one's own opinion but without taking full responsibility for it. Once an opinion expressed in the group is accepted by the group, it has found a majority. Should the judgment subsequently turn out to be wrong, then the blame can be divided between several people. If, on the other hand, the opinion is correct, then it is often experienced as an individual achievement on the part of group members.

Typical market participant group for heart people
It is now clear where heart people can be found in the financial markets: everywhere where there are groups and where decisions are preferably taken jointly. This includes not only situations in which a compromise is sought by voting for the various positions

---

[5] We deliberately have not discussed group behavior and the decision-making processes in groups. Please see Auer-Rizzi (1998) for further details.

put forward by decision makers in a company, but also the relationship between a consultant and his client.

Decisions that are arrived at by several people cannot, by definition, be subject to a short-term timeframe. The search for suitable discussion partners, the discussions themselves, and the follow-up evaluation all take time. Only gut people are short-term oriented, as essentially only they decide spontaneously, i.e. they enter and thus liquidate exposures independently. An exclusively long-term point of view, however, does not apply to heart people. This would mean that the success or failure of a decision could not be established within a reasonable period. However, social groups or contacts – say, a relationship between consultant and client – do not last forever. Otherwise feedback, which is so important to heart people, such as praise and being loved, would be out of the question. At the same time, however, it is clear that the number of social contacts is greatest in the case of a medium-term timeframe. The short-term day trader can maintain control only when engaged in intensive trading if other people do not disturb him, while the long-term investor enters the market only once and from then on is hardly interested in conversations on this subject. The typical planning horizon for heart people or for the emotional market participant is therefore the medium term.

Market participants with a medium-term timeframe include companies that import or export goods or services from abroad. Their main aim is to insure against currency movements on the foreign exchanges. They are faced with the choice, for instance, of insuring themselves against future currency movements by concluding a forward transaction, or by exploiting a current trend to make a profit, if a contract is invoiced in a foreign currency. In the first case, the exporter or importer acquires a clear basis for calculation in respect of the expected revenue from a sale or the goods or services bought abroad. He has decided not to run a currency risk and will therefore be resigned to the outcome of future market developments, if he is not bothered about foregoing a possible profit.

Insuring against currency movements is therefore similar to hedging an open position. Without the forward trade, for instance if the importer or exporter expects a favorable currency movement, the position is similar to an open trading position. Often, several people in a firm's currency management division are involved in the decision as to whether to hedge a currency risk or to leave it open – the responsibility is divided amongst several people. This has the advantage that decisions do not depend on any one individual (and their psychological inclination), but there is also the serious disadvantage that important measures are possibly taken too late. This occurs particularly if the group is too large, and relevant decision-making majorities can therefore not be found quickly enough, or if the group meets only from time to time, so that important changes are missed in a volatile market.

Something similar applies to investment funds and asset managers, where trading decisions are often made by investment committees, i.e. by groups. In addition, investment funds can also have speculation as a motive for trading, as well as the investment aspect. The managers of the fund are faced with emotions similar to the short-term trader when investing in an individual investment, but they will be able to handle these in a different way to solitary traders (who can rely only on themselves) as they also usually make their decisions in groups, which often respond slowly to changes in the market.

The pressure to perform, exerted by competition from other investment funds, is also high. Although daily comparisons are possible, the intervals between which investment funds are compared with each other are nevertheless greater than in the case of short-term traders. Monthly or even annual yields usually determine the attraction or otherwise of an investment fund.

Many private investors belong to the group of medium-term market participants, as they do not wish to act as short-term speculators, nor do they have the patience to deploy exclusively a robust long-term strategy. This group does not decide individually: decisions are usually taken in consultation with others, either in investment clubs or informally amongst friends. These investors are supported in particular by their financial advisors, who generally also employ a medium-term timeframe.

Financial advisors can be distinguished in one important point from private investors: they themselves invest not at all or only to a limited extent in the markets. Nevertheless, they also have an interest in the correctness or otherwise of their advice. Advisors are often more disappointed when their advice turns out to be incorrect than the client. The financial advisor therefore pursues not only material interests, but also other objectives. For instance, he likes to build and preserve a reputation, or to be acclaimed. Negatively, he might be envious of the success of others.

Susceptibility profile of emotional market participants
It is characteristic for heart people that they will try to reinforce positive feelings and suppress negative ones to a large degree. They therefore need success, and the success or failure of an exposure depends on the purchase price. That is why the purchase price is important for heart people. Unlike gut people, who identify more or less exclusively with the purchase price, heart people gather large amounts of news through the many contacts they maintain, and are therefore always supplied with information. The purchase price nevertheless plays a large role in the self-esteem of heart people because the success of an exposure can be measured only against the purchase price. Heart people need success in order to find the sympathy and recognition vital for them within the group.

The greatest weakness of heart people lies in their absolute need for harmony. Anything that might disturb or reduce this harmony, even slightly, will be avoided. They typically avoid dissonance, and they will admit only reluctantly that they have made mistakes. They are emotionally committed to a wrong decision, and look for opportunities to make the best of a difficult situation (dissonance). Heart people are therefore inclined to resort to selective observation: they prefer information that confirms their transaction or their opinion, and simultaneously they ignore all unfavorable news or play it down. They do this in particular in the presence of others, for there is one thing they avoid at all costs: to be the messenger of bad news, or to be unloved. Moreover, they find it hard to admit that they must have done something wrong in connection with an exposure, as they set so much emotional store by their decisions. This commitment increases greatly if there are many witnesses to the transaction, as is the case within a group.

As heart types avoid dissonance, they will hesitate a long time before realizing their losses in the case of unfavorable market developments. The heart person feels accountable to himself, so he watches his position go from bad to worse without doing anything, until there is no hope. He lets the exposure run and wipes it from his memory, as long as the loss is not too great. He may not get his investment back for several years – perhaps not at all.

Even without personal exposure in the market, there is the ideal commitment to one's self. This is always the case with a financial advisor, as generally they should not trade, at least not in the market on which they advise.[6] Immaterial commitments, for instance in the form of a market opinion, can be risky in certain circumstances, as they may give rise to immaterial losses in the case of opinion leaders, but also material losses amongst the "young ones". Opinions based on logic are particularly resistant to radical changes, which might be similar to the realization of a loss. In addition, there is the regret of having changed horses at exactly the wrong time. Such "paper losses" are therefore often played down by emotional actors.

Losses are very painful for heart types, and they are usually aware of this even before their exposure. So it is not surprising that emotional market participants are somewhat anxious. Transactions for which the risk cannot be calculated, or that depart greatly from "normal" exposures, must be avoided at all costs. Shares from their own country are considered preferable to foreign stocks. The thought of entering into an unfortunate transaction abroad, or to have to justify it, leads them to avoid such transactions from the start. If, on the other hand, the blue-chip stock did not do very well, then they know they are in good company.

Figure 6-4 shows a susceptibility profile for a heart person. The greatest difficulty lies in the fact that the heart person sets too

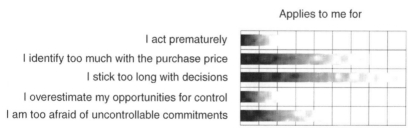

Figure 6-4 Typical susceptibility profile for an emotional market participant.

---

[6] Clients might be impressed if an advisor underlines his trading ideas with personal transactions. Unfortunately, this also means that information that confirms the exposure (irrespective of whether it is large or small – the point is to get it right) will be filtered.

much store by his decisions, which, together with his strong identification with purchase prices, leads to a clear manifestation of the
disposition effect. Heart people also turn out to be comparatively
anxious market participants.

Headstrong: the rational type

Many people think themselves clever, particularly in relation to
money. It is also difficult for individuals to make purely rational
decisions, as people continuously receive signals from the "heart"
that sabotage this. So, when we speak of a person who is rationally
inclined, we mean a thinking, practical type – a "head person":
someone who, in the first instance, is controlled by the neocortex.

The head person tends to perceive dangers early and frequently,
and his greatest fear is to not know enough to spot and avert these
dangers. This also includes the fear of making wrong decisions,
which may be so great that he sometimes postpones decisions for
as long as possible, or does not make them at all. The status quo
would seem to be the most secure situation, for he knows it well,
while departures from the norm are undertaken with the utmost
reluctance.

The main motive for head people is therefore reduction of the
fear of uncertainty. In order to achieve this, they try to control the
factors that may influence the uncertain future. They will weigh up
the interrelationships and effects of their actions on the basis of
reason. They therefore require a rational explanation for everything. They would prefer to model all future behavior. As the basic
principle, "knowledge is power", applies to them, they are inquisit-
ive and essentially more willing to learn than the gut or heart types.
Head people will not rest until they have found an explanation for
everything, even if initially it seems completely illogical, and even
if they have to reason away facts that conflict with their interpretation.

This practical type does not like sweeping changes in his
environment unless the change is considered to be rational and
makes sense. Head people have difficulty letting go of something
they have grown fond of: letting go could mean loss of control. In
extreme cases, this characteristic can grow into an obsession, so

that everything must be controlled – nothing unforeseen must take place. It is therefore not surprising that many head types prefer to pass their days in isolation. They will only join others if they have a similar outlook. Head people often gather in small groups. They value not the social contacts, but the perceived gains in control through an increased supply of information or comparison of information and opinions.

Typical market participation groups for head people
Head people would very much like to control the development of prices in the financial markets themselves. As they know they cannot exert such control, they will at least try to control factors that could influence future behavior of market participants: all information and forecasts. They do this by collecting as much information as possible. Naturally, they would prefer to compile the forecasts themselves, because nobody can do it better (in order to retain control).

Head types are found mostly amongst analysts. They do not mix with gut and heart people, and they try to observe the market from a (secure) distance. They are not inclined to short-term speculation. Analysts typically are not responsible for positions, nor do they wish to be. This applies to most economists in banks – as fundamental analysts – as well as for technically oriented analysts. The fact that the latter in particular often do not trade themselves is surprising, as generally technical forecasts are practical predictions that are actually tradable, in contrast to forecasts issued by economically oriented analysts. Analysts enter into positions themselves only when they are absolutely sure, and this requires a lot of preparation and information. Head people will have developed, tested and optimized their own trading systems over a long period of time before they actually use them for their own transactions.

Head people are also found amongst long-term investors. The trading motive of these market participants is not a quick profit but a steady, far-reaching certain increase in capital: investments that are generally held for years, possibly decades. The long-term investor will avidly collect comprehensive information in order to decide where to invest. He may wait a long time before he actually becomes active in the market. He manages to satisfy his manifest need for control through his long-term view. He is willing to take a risk when he realizes that his investments may not do so well in the short term, but they are secure in the long term.

Typical susceptibility profile of the practical market participant
Head people in the markets aim in the first instance to produce income over the long term, in a sustained way. They are not concerned primarily with making a fast buck, but rather with a possible risk-free profit. If they cannot achieve this objective without some degree of risk, then the risk must at least be controllable.

They always remain on the safe side, with exposures that they can actually control (or that they believe they can control). They are also usually prepared to run greater risks in the case of larger positions in order to improve their performance. This greater risk, however, is not based on carelessness, as in the case of gut people. Head people, unlike gut people, make sure that they are well-informed. There is no question of overestimating control opportunities or of a control illusion in this case.

Head people will give situations a wide berth if they cannot see the overall picture and fear losing control. There is one thing that they do not like: suddenly having to cope with powerful feelings, such as fear (in the case of a control deficit) or panic (in the case of total loss of control). Head people therefore have a deep-seated aversion towards entering into exposures that are difficult to control. On the whole, they trade infrequently, or they may not invest in the financial markets at all. This indicates their greatest susceptibility to one of the five rationality instances. For without trading there is no profit.

When head people become active, there is a risk that they will experience a control deficit in the case of an unexpected price development, accompanied by painful feelings of being at the mercy of something as a result of their extreme need for control. They will then do their utmost to regain control of the market by seeking confirmation from other actors or analysts that they did not act on the basis of false conclusions. They will believe themselves to be masters of the situation, again on the basis of biased information. Head people will naturally seek confirmation in the location where it will be offered to them, i.e. they will try to get information that supports their way of thinking. It is likely that

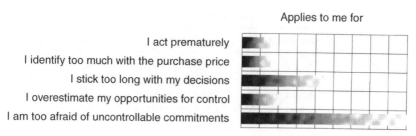

Figure 6-5 Typical susceptibility profile of a practical market participant.

they will look for – and find – similar-minded analysts or others. At worst, they will agree that the markets have again been irrational and could not be predicted.

Large profits or losses may accumulate over a long period, without head people changing their opinions or investment behavior. Losses in particular are often sat out over periods of many years, sometimes even across generations. The same applies to profits on paper, which may only be realized following an inheritance. Exposures, on the other hand, are often cleared only in the case of comparatively quick and unexpectedly large gains.

Figure 6-5 shows that head people hold back too much in the financial markets, due to their manifest need for control. They miss lucrative opportunities that they may have discovered for themselves through careful analysis, due to their risk aversion. In addition, they are fully committed to their decisions, as is clear from the fact that they will only seek out information that confirms their judgment, and block out all other messages. But they are not inclined to overestimate their opportunities for control, nor do they act prematurely in most cases. As practical market participants are often committed in the long term, they do not identify too much with the purchase price.

Table 6-1 gives an overview of the three types of market participant. It may seem somewhat bold to present such a strict classification, but we are not saying that all traders are gut people, or that all analysts are head people: the fact that most people are a blend of types, with one type dominant, makes this impossible. Nor should time horizons be assigned to individual types of market participant on the basis of an inflexible classification. There may well be actors

Table 6-1   The three types of market participant

	Gut person	Heart person	Head person
Typical group	Traders Day traders Short-term investors	Financial advisors Asset managers Fund managers Currency managers Medium-term investors	Analysts Long-term investors
Preferred time horizon	Short term	Medium term	Long term
Main motive	Quick results Preserving what has been achieved	Freedom of dissonance	Control
Particularly susceptible to	Heuristics Identification with purchase prices Control illusion	Selective observation Committed to decisions	Avoidance of fear Selective observation

who are active within more than one time window at a time. Or exposures originally considered to be short term may subsequently enter a loss situation and be converted into long-term strategic positions. Or investments originally planned as long-term stock holdings may show a large profit after only a short time, so they are realized immediately. Finally, the trading horizon of an actor need not necessarily indicate his character, i.e. a short-term investor need not be a gut person, and not every market participant with a long-term view is necessarily a head person.

Chapter 7

Free advice

Valuable tips for successful trades

We have explained why people cannot always make rational decisions. We have showed how people use heuristics to help solve problems quickly in the case of complex decision-making situations, but that this does not always lead to the right solution. Problems in observation, processing and the evaluation of information often play tricks on people. It is doubtful whether such conclusions ultimately lead to the best solutions. Moreover, people are systematically influenced by motives underlying dissonance distortion and the need for control when observing and judging.

In Chapter 2 we described a currency trader entering a position. His intuition, mind and emotions governed his actions. He made a profit on his first transaction, which he quickly realized. Further positions also had a positive outcome. His self-confidence and courage increased with continued success. At the same time, the trader no longer studied the information received from others in the same detail; in fact, he became quite careless over time. The pleasure in making a profit could therefore be termed "experienced consonance", and the euphoria ultimately defined as the result of complete control illusion.

When prices slowly but steadily move in the wrong direction, it is not just the initial optimism that disappears – the hope that everything will turn out right in the end. Rather, the first signs of fear become visible when losses reach a certain order of magnitude, resulting from a decrease in control. This deficit is initially reduced by searching out favorable information and forecasts. People will mutually reassure each other, reiterating what everyone already knows. Unfortunately, these conversations merely have a tranquillizing effect: they reduce dissonance. The risks and side effects of reducing dissonance are given in Chapter 5.

The outlook is especially bad for market participants who have entered a particularly large position based on a previous run of successes – just like the trader in Chapter 2. Intoxicated by a sense of his own power, and spurred on by total control illusion, he could not at first understand what was happening. The conviction that he was right again completely clouded his sense of reality. Only slowly (usually after a number of sobering losses) did he become aware of a control deficit, at which point he was overcome by paralyzing fear.

The perception of the trader changed at the stage when everything pleaded against his position. Instead of liquidating his commitment, he suppressed all unfavorable news and information and exaggerated positive reports. He perceived selectively. He attached too much value to a small recovery, which initially reduced the threatening loss. The control deficit suddenly decreased along with the dissonance. It then seemed justified to "improve" the bid or offer price with additional transactions at the now more favorable price. The courage for such a deed was generated by relief at regaining control.

Once the position began to look bad again, our market participant came up against another looming control deficit, if not complete loss of control, upon prices reaching a new low. This resulted in panic. He finally managed to withdraw from the situation by liquidating the entire position. The control deficit clearly proved too large and had become unbearable.

The course of this transaction is by no means an exception. Rather, it is an example of the main risks of irrational behavior. Not all (trading) days and positions are identical, but there are many similarities. We will show here the distortions and risks that await market participants in many situations on the basis of an arbitrary transaction. We will offer advice as to how market participants can make the best of any situation and increase their profits. The tips should be regarded as support rather than cautionary tales.

The process of trading will be divided into the four stages of motivation, information, transaction and overcoming dissonance, so as to offer a systematic overview of the effect of the scientific findings discussed in previous chapters on market participant behavior.

The explanations are again related to examples in the currency market, which is known not only for its transparency. Moreover, this is a market in which supply and demand is balanced if there is high liquidity. The examples can therefore be applied without any difficulty to stock, bonds, commodity and futures markets.

WHAT MOTIVATES ACTORS?

The motives that lead people to participate in a market might, at first glance, seem to be numerous, but this is not the case. Ultimately, the objective of closing transactions successfully is the only motive that matters. Whether we are dealing with a commodity, service or financial market, all participants want to exchange something and make a profit. They want to buy goods at a favorable price in order to consume them, for investment purposes, or to sell them at a higher price. Services and labor are also offered at the highest achievable price, in order to buy other goods and services with the money received, or to invest the capital in the financial markets at a profit. The latter is determined in the first instance by the objective to maximize net profit (Mann 1994).

This also applies to actors in the currency markets, e.g. an investor in foreign shares who requires foreign currency to pay for them, an exporter who wants to or must convert revenue from selling goods or services, or a short-term market participant who buys a currency intending to sell it later at a profit, and who is often considered to be a speculator. The term "speculator" stems from the Latin *speculari*, meaning "looking out". In this case, the spectator is looking out for profitable openings. Basically, all market participants are engaged in speculation, even when they wish only to hedge against unforeseen price fluctuations through a futures contract. Holding off and hoping for a better opportunity is also a form of speculation.

Most people imagine that market participants have only one motive – maximizing profit. But take a man who has never had anything to do with the financial markets. One day, his neighbor comes home in an expensive car. The man cannot understand how his neighbor can afford it, as they have similar salaries. It soon becomes clear that the $100,000 car is not just hired. A win on the lottery or an inheritance are also ruled out after some initial probing. The neighbour whispers something incomprehensible about writing options, about a large leverage, about volatility. The man asks himself, "What can he do that I can't?" The answer has led many to the stock exchange.

Be clear about how you measure success before entering a transaction. Are you seeking an amount of money, a particular yield, or enjoyment, or do you just want to be proven right?

Envy of neighbors, colleagues or friends is at the bottom of many transactions. Even the desire to look clever can be a motive to enter into commitments that might merely yield many quick profits, instead of a high return: many small gains are often offset by a single loss. The hit rate is therefore enticingly high. The fact that the many gains are often more than offset by a single bad loss is withheld.

Always check your motive for trading. You want to maximize profits and minimize losses. Do not listen to other actors or friends, because they will invariably tell you only of their successes. It is your money, and only you should determine how it should grow.

Anyone who plays the markets professes a point of view, an opinion or a prediction at the point at which he opens a position. Predictions are in great demand, as these offer (subjective) information about the probable outcome of a transaction. Similarly, the performance by the actor, expressed in profit or loss, becomes measurable and comparable to the performance of others, as well as to the market as a whole. This situation lasts for as long as the position remains open and ends only when it is completely liquidated. Only then does it become clear whether the trader is a winner or a loser.

A lot of time may pass before this point is reached. Most people experience difficulty with this aspect, and many tend to end this state of uncertainty, clearing the position as soon as they have made a paper profit. Traders tend to be influenced by the subliminal fear that profits accumulating slower than expected could be destroyed quickly and suddenly, despite their initial pleasure. On the other hand, if profits rise quickly over a comparatively short period of time – often by chance through price shocks – then the inclination is to believe that such price developments take place so seldom and are so extraordinary that it is not likely to occur again in the near future. They overestimate the price reversal compared to a possible additional yield, so that the position is liquidated. Time therefore represents a risk of losing what has already been gained in the case of a positive development of a transaction.

On the other hand, imagine how painful a transaction threatening a loss must be, as the defeat cannot, or will not, be admitted. The hope that with time everything will come right always raises its head. This happens in particular with paper losses, which arise slowly, as players continue to believe that a rapid trend reversal will save the day. If, however, the adverse price development takes place disproportionately quickly, then people will not believe that a similar movement will occur again before too long, as in the case of a positive price shock. They are therefore not usually willing to realize the loss at that time, as the risk of getting out at what may be the lowest price seems disproportionately high.

Don't be fooled by the time factor in relation to your open positions. Profits developing reluctantly need not be a sign of imminent loss. Similarly, losses arising slowly are not a sign of imminent profit.

Traders are thus confronted with two imponderable factors before they decide to enter into a position. They must predict the future direction of price movements, and they must be able to estimate correctly the period of time that elapses before the forecast becomes true. They will not only use fundamental or technical (forecast) methods in order to solve this problem; they will blend these with their very own experiences, common sense judgment and the general market expectation of future price developments.

The time or forecast horizon of a market participant also plays an essential role. The longer the forecast period, the less reliable the forecast, as the probability that new events may arise after the position has been entered increases with time. New information and its presentation play vital roles. This problem is usually solved by analysts who are involved in the decision-making process by dividing their forecasts into different forecast horizons of short-, medium- and long-term analyses. It is only natural that they are more generous in the case of long-term predictions than in the case of next-day predictions.

INFORMATION = RUINATION?

There is a great need for analyses and forecasts, as well as information, before making important decisions in the financial markets, as they help save time. Analyses summarize processed and condensed information. The demand for information and analyses is based on the basic human need for control. This need is particularly strong in the financial markets, where there are new winners and losers every day. As traders know only too well, today's hero can very quickly become tomorrow's loser. And nobody likes being a loser.

The desire to collect as much information as possible arises some time before entering a position, and accompanies traders for the entire period the position is open, until it has been liquidated. Even then, there might still be the need for an explanation and assimilation of what happened. Yet fully informed market participants are not exactly common. The more a participant believes himself to be informed, however, the more he will be convinced that he controls the situation. Information available to the actor includes external data relating to the market and reported political events, and internal information, such as the balance of his own account, i.e. profits and losses. Once a position is in the profit zone, it generates a feeling of pleasure and satisfaction in the market participant, and the impression that he has full control of his position by taking the right steps. His need for control may have been met to such an extent that he believes any further information to be superfluous. The sense of invincibility grows once he has been successful several times in a row; the feeling of euphoria may even prevent him from taking note of relevant facts and data.

> Do not become careless in relation to information and analyses, even if you believe you are in control. Pretend you have not yet decided to enter the position.

The reverse applies to losses, when the need for control will automatically increase. Traders will seek out information that justifies the present situation, if not the original decision, and puts it in a better light. The (illusory) knowledge of factors influencing a decision-making situation can help to regain the control believed to be lost, at least temporarily.

> Look for information that runs counter to your commitment, even if this proves difficult. At the same time, question information that confirms your original decision.

Information, and processing it, up to the moment of the decision is the most important and influential aspect that affects day-to-day trading in the financial markets, especially in relation to the subsequent cash price of a transaction. Information processing is a controversial area in scientific circles. The basic principles of modern financial markets theory, which can be traced back to the "efficient market hypothesis", assume that market participants behave in a strictly rational manner. Their decisions are assumed to be always based on information that has been fully assimilated – as a consequence, the majority of actors respond similarly to new messages and events.

Yet we learned in Chapter 3 that people are systematically at risk of errors, misunderstandings and false conclusions in the perception of information, as well as in its assimilation. In other words, these are not just occasional instances that are offset by the other "rational" market participants, or phenomena of mass euphoria or panic. Rational thinking and acting requires that the actor has access to accurate and essential information, and that he recognizes and perceives it as such (Maas and Weibler 1990a). In fact, material investment might be required in certain circumstances in order to acquire important information and data, and not every market participant is prepared to do this. Such information includes up-to-date prices furnished by news agencies at the same time as market activities.

Not all participants in the markets have access to the same news and information. Short-term traders may well be at an advantage compared with other groups – at least in relation to the amount of information available. They normally have at least one online connection with a news agency. On the other hand, there is also the time pressure. News information must be absorbed and assimilated extremely rapidly in trading firms. There is no time to reflect on the content and weigh up the consequences for hours, as market prices often move in seconds – especially when the incoming information was contrary to expectation. In general, traders are inclined to simplify complex information. This often results in unexplained price shocks, which are not corrected until later, following detailed examination of news. But it cannot be assumed that positions, entered as a result of the misinterpretation, will be liquidated again following fresh information.

Avoid a surfeit of information: information = ruination. Concentrate on the most relevant information, and analyze it in detail.

Medium-term market participants also have good access to the main information issued by news agencies, insofar as they are connected online. However, prepared or filtered information from brokers or analysts is not online, and there is a risk that part of the news will be lost. Sometimes, information reaches the recipient so late that it has no more value than the paper it is printed on. A consultant who has just entered a proprietory position may seek out information that confirms his commitment, and as a result he will pass on only that type of information. On the other hand, the medium-term actor has considerably more time at his disposal for the evaluation of information.

If possible, ask for advice only from analysts and brokers who have not entered a position in the market segment you are interested in. An advisor who has his own market position to consider might feed you only that information that justifies his own commitment.

Long-term private investors usually have more time at their disposal for absorbing and assimilating information than other market participants. This is, however, not always comprehensive. Most are satisfied with the financial section of a daily newspaper or a TV business program. Other people will rely on the financial advisor with a bank they trust. They may surf the Web for the latest events and background information, which is, incidentally, a good opportunity to get close to sources of information.

Remember that information, recommendations and secret tips have usually been around for a while. Other market participants may well have positioned themselves already, so that a real change in supply and demand is no longer expected.

Communicating information

As a result of the surfeit of information, people need to select information that is relevant to them, even when the individual pieces of information are supposed to have a simple structure. The opportunities for assimilating information that are available to the trader are either of an acoustic or visual nature. Misunderstandings can occur early on in the acoustic process, through slips of the tongue, language barriers or simply by mishearing what was said. Mishearing a number, for instance an important economic statistic such as the US unemployment figure or the size of an increase or drop in interest, may lead to dramatic consequences.

The response time to information in the case of short-term market participants is often only fractions of seconds, as only the fastest actor will get the supposedly best price.

A message that is loud and clear is likely to be more important than information that can hardly be heard or is unclear for other reasons. Information in this context also includes market prices. Although the number of brokers in the currency trade has fallen considerably in recent years, they still have a considerable influence on the future behavior of actors. The deafening shouts with which brokers announce a jump in price contain additional information: the mood. The excited voice of the broker gives the impression that something is happening in the market, of which the trader is not yet aware, and he may ask himself anxiously, "What is it the others know that I don't?"

Concentrate on the core of the matter, as far as your decisions are concerned. Do not let your attention be diverted from the actual problem at issue by news that you have just heard or propaganda.

On the other hand, information may be overlooked completely because it falls below the perception threshold of market participants, which means the physical stimulus (e.g. the volume of a TV broadcast) is too low for the recipient. Information that is not sufficiently loud to be heard in a trading office is not perceived by other traders, as the level of noise emitted by equipment, telephones, conversations between colleagues, and other sources is already relatively high. Important information may therefore get lost amongst the general background noise.

Risks inherent in availability and selective observation

The complexity of many pieces of information has a deterrent effect, which can sometimes prevent assimilation. Expressions such as, "I'm not a scientist", "That's why we have analysts", or "I can't do everything" must not be interpreted as plain excuses or laziness; rather, they are the result of a certain lack of power. The inability to assimilate complex information brings with it the risk of shortening and distorting messages that are directed at market participants, which will lead almost certainly to wrong decisions. This applies not only to short-term traders, but also to those actors who have more time at their disposal. Decisions must be made as quickly as possible and with the least amount of effort.

Participants in the financial markets tend to reduce perceived complexity in decision-making situations by using certain heuristics. Availability plays an important role here. Information that is easily available is absorbed more often than information that is difficult to access, irrespective of the extent of the relevance. Topicality also plays a role, as new information is easier to recall from memory and the media.

Remember, news that is easily accessible to you is usually also easily available for other actors. There is every likelihood that it has already been traded, i.e. that the news is already reflected in the market price.

Memory also has an effect on the availability of events, especially when the events can be recalled without difficulty. The livelier and more colorfully they were perceived, the easier they will be recalled. For instance, when facing an important decision, you may remember the colleague who sold his shares at the right time, multiplied his capital by a factor of ten by purchasing options, and invited you to an expensive dinner to celebrate. The evaluation of the current situation is influenced by precisely such personal impressions. The estimation of the probability of future events or gains or losses is therefore often based on subjective and prejudiced memories.

A typical example of such memories can be found in the currency trade, where there is often talk of "natural bulls" or "natural bears", i.e. market participants who always bet on rising respectively falling prices out of principle. These convictions stem from the first successful phase that they experienced as active participants in the market. Traders who succeed big time during a sustained uptrend (e.g. the US dollar during the period 1980–85, are bound to never forget this time. Actors who earned their first spurs during a serious downward trend (e.g. the US dollar in the period 1986–88) are permanently affected by these events, which may well influence the assimilation of information.

Try to seek out people whose opinions of the market, or another economic situation, differ from yours.

The media contribute considerably to the effect of these personal impressions. People will, in the first instance, try to obtain analyses and commentary that correspond most to the current mood of the public, even when selecting market information for a public offering on the stock exchange. Pessimists are not in demand – except as a deterrent. An estimation as to the probability of a particular event taking place can be influenced by drawing or diverting the attention. New emissions of shares whose price exceeds the emission price by 50 or 100 per cent on the day they are floated on the stock exchange are a typical example. When even the evening news reports on the extraordinary event, many people will say, "I won't miss out next time."

Do not respond to every bit of news you hear. Keep your eye on the big picture, on the basis of which you may have made a decision.

Availability also plays a large role in relation to the estimation of future risks of currency, stock etc. The risk of high volatility is generally overestimated after a hectic trading day with violent price fluctuations, while the risks are regularly underestimated in the case of quiet markets. People do not expect a market that has hardly moved for months to suddenly explode. Even small fluctuations will be overvalued, due to either fear or joy, when they occur against expectation. Again, people will only recall the recent past, in which the market was perceived to be "dead".

Reality shows us, however, that, particularly after periods of high volatility (expressed by the standard deviation from previous prices), the trades of market participants are considerably reduced, as the fear for further violent fluctuations prevails. This will normally cause the volatility of the prices to be reduced, which ultimately should lead to quieter times in the market. In quiet times, when prices hardly move, a trader must enter comparatively large positions, in order to earn at least a little money. Imagine what happens when such a market suddenly takes off.

The effect of availability can be seen in many areas of judgment on the part of market participants. Actors often have an exaggerated idea of the number of people who share their opinions. This false judgment, also called "false consensus", is explained in particular by the fact that personal convictions (typically, market rules of thumb) can be recalled very easily from memory. These opinions are considered to be easily realized, "normal" and therefore widespread (Bierhoff 1993). The personal opinion of certain situations therefore also influences its judgment. When you then encounter two or three similarly minded trading colleagues, there is immediately a question of a clear majority ("everyone says so"), which strengthens the sense of control. On the other hand, if a trader comes across market participants or analysts with different views, then the trader will usually simply ignore them. This applies particularly when the content of the information is ambivalent. The same message will probably be perceived differently by different people: an optimist will see the latest US economic statistics in a different light to a pessimist.

Don't be deceived: market participants who agree with your analysis often hold the same position as you and are therefore in a similar frame of mind.

Availability may lead to a disregard of possibly important information. Selective observation has a similar effect, as perception on the part of market participants is often affected strongly by their personal experience. They are, to all intents and purposes, prejudiced. Traders and investors in particular tend to overvalue information that agrees with their own ideas. There is also a tendency to suppress, or even to ignore, such information if it does not fit one's personal image of the world. This selective perception often occurs subconsciously and is usually unintentional. Irregularities in the presentation of information are often not heard or seen, or they are simply "made to fit", especially if communicated under pressure of time.

Analysts are also selective in their perception of information and events, even though they usually do not operate under the same pressure of time as traders. They seek out what fits their theoretical and personal preconceived views of the world (Hunter and Coggin 1988) from the large number of data and news messages. At the same time, the need for control, which in this group of market participants (head people) is usually particularly strong, is met. As such attitudes vary from analyst to analyst, each has an individual perception spectrum. We should not assume that all analysts apply the same criteria to the selection and evaluation of information. They will therefore arrive at different conclusions. The data that they consider relevant will be attributed a disproportionally large weight, which may result in distortions in their predictions. In particular, information that has already been perceived and assimilated is perceived as more favorable. Even information absorbed incidentally – without people being aware of its effect – may influence the later assimilation of information (Felser 1997).

Technically oriented analysts in particular often fall victim to selective observation. Chart analysis requires a certain skill in relation to pattern recognition, therefore people are tempted to look only for certain configurations, in particular, those that fit the often preconceived market picture. When tracing trend lines, technical analysts often select lines with multiple changes of direction. The fact that other trend lines were often not sustained is played down subconsciously, or even ignored.

Cyclical methods in technical analysis, for instance the Elliott Wave Theory, function especially well on paper. The theory is not quite so successful when the forecasts are compared with actual trades. It is, of course, possible that the downwards correction in a market equals exactly 61.8 per cent (a so-called Fibonacci retracement) of the preceding upwards movement, in which case the theory has been proven right once again. The fact that the market has previously breached other main correction levels is not mentioned. As long as the analyst does not need to trade, he can afford the luxury of cherry picking hits only. Insinuating that someone who does not earn any money using the Elliot Wave Theory or Gann cycli has not understood these theories correctly is going too far, however.

Risks inherent in anchoring

As short-term market participants are often under pressure of time, they need to assimilate new information as quickly and as economically as possible. But actors with medium- or even long-term trading horizons often give themselves too little time to process information thoroughly.

Anchoring and adaptation is therefore used in the first instance when particular information cannot be assembled and judged immediately by participants in the financial markets. In that case, they will tend to orient themselves on a source or reference value (anchor) when evaluating it, in order to draw conclusions from it at a later stage. These reference values are normally set by experts, such as economists and analysts. The anchors need not necessarily be numerical values; they can also be based on opinions or views (for instance from friends or experts). Anchor values play an important role before the publication of important economic data, as traders often do not have much time to devote to the evaluation. In fact, traders are often not clear about the effect important statistics will have on prices just hours before publication. Simple, easily judged estimates that facilitate the judging of data without having to think long and hard about them are in demand. These forecasts are usually compiled from the average of several polls, which few people understand exactly how they are produced.

When the "median" for the US balance of trade for month x shows a deficit of $11.2 billion, this merely means that it is an average of all estimates amongst analysts questioned. Whether these analysts are good or bad, whether the respondent was the economist manager or a clerk, cannot be traced. The median is often supplemented by a forecast from the company conducting the poll, for instance a deficit of $12.5 billion. People may therefore assume that a band of $11.2–12.5 billion will be used as an anchor for subsequent decisions.

Should the forecast band be exceeded positively in this situation, then the advice is to buy commodities, shares, currencies and other tradables for which it can be assumed that the fundamental data in question will have a favorable effect. If, on the other hand, the figure remains below the forecast, then people will sell. This is a considerable simplification. The following situation could arise if the band predicted above for the US balance of trade deficit ($11.2–12.5 billion) is applied to the currency trade:

Figures that are below $11.2 billion are better than expected and are therefore interpreted as favorable for the future of the US dollar by market participants. Should the actual deficit exceed $12.5 billion, then this will be regarded as unfavorable for the US economy. Assuming that the published figure is $10.7 billion, then traders will, for instance, buy dollars against the euro. After all, the figure is better than expected. The fact that it may still be a bad statistic for the USA is overlooked. As a result, the quality of the forecasts by economists questioned previously, rather than the fundamental data, is traded. The economists' task in this case is to forecast as exactly as possible.

Do not rely on a single anchor value. Remember that many anchors are set deliberately in order to generate a particular opinion. Balance particularly optimistic forecasts against particularly pessimistic opinions. Expect the unexpected.

Anchoring also plays an important role for analysts. For example, an analyst who has been asked for the price of the euro in three months' time will proceed as follows: Several plausible forecast values are considered, e.g. the futures price. They will then choose the figure that seems to be clearest. As the analyst does not want to be pinned down to a point forecast (i.e. to the forecast of an exact figure of, say, $1.0500), he will try to indicate a band (e.g. $1.0250–1.0750) around the figure. The calculation of such a band, however, is merely an adaptation process as part of the anchoring heuristic, which we know is often too low. The band will, therefore, often be too narrow.

The analyst faces a dilemma. If he makes the band too wide (say, $0.9500–1.1500), then his forecast will be classed as worthless, as the information content equals zero. If he makes the band too narrow, then the risk of a getting it wrong is greater. The main thing in the world of everyday trading is that the forecast is as meaningful as possible, without exposing the analyst too much, so as not to risk his reputation if he gets it wrong. Also, the analyst will receive an immediate reward for an informative forecast, for the recipients will act on it. The accuracy of the prediction can be shown only at the end of the period covered by the forecast (Yaniv and Foster 1997). But for many of the recipients, there has been too much water under the bridge, so the quality of the forecast is no longer relevant to them. Most will have long forgotten what the analyst said. In other words, decisions made on the basis of the forecast may well have been revised in the meantime. The analyst is therefore cheated out of his just reward unless we are dealing with very short-term forecasts. In response, he can only say, "Look, I was right that time".

The probability of the predicted numbers falling within the estimated band, i.e. the certainty of the prediction, is also of interest to the user. People tend to have a disproportionate amount of trust in their own capability, which systematically generates distortions, as shown in Chapter 5. In practice, this also supports the effect mentioned above, that forecast bands are often too narrow.[1]

Assume that analysts set most forecast bands too narrowly. Compare actual bands on the basis of historic price data for a currency, stock etc. over a specific period in order to arrive at more realistic values.

Comparing opinions, often practiced by short-term market participants due to time pressure, leads to anchoring. The comparison takes place at the start of trading, as the latest news and events will not yet have been processed. It is, of course, much easier to call a friend and ask him for his views. The answer is often ill-considered, due to lack of time, or may be colored by subjective first impressions, in particular when the person called has his own position to consider. For instance, when asked about news regarding the euro/US dollar, the response will generally be distorted if the actor has just taken a position with regard to the currency. He will then try to justify his transaction, even if this is not immediately obvious to others, and argue in favor of it. In the case of a long-term

[1] The fact that overconfidence can also affect experienced experts' own judgment is shown by Kiell and Stephan's 1997 experiment with brokers. Subjects were asked to predict some share and currency prices, accompanied by forecast bands with 90 per cent confidence intervals. Only 24 per cent of the 360 forecasts issued were right, instead of the 90 per cent required.

position, the person questioned will usually pass on information that underwrites his decision. As he has staked on rising prices, he will emphasize positive news and underplay or withhold contradictory information. The subjective information will, in any case, serve as an anchor for the player, which he will qualify only to a small extent.

Avoid confirming your opinion, information and analyses by a third party who holds the same position as yourself.

The observation of "round" price levels, such as a euro price of $1.0000, 1.1000 or even 1.3000, is related to anchoring. Such levels are also popularly considered to be psychologically important milestones, although they normally only have a temporary effect on prices, as prices will remain exactly at these levels only in the most exceptional cases. Generally, a change in the first decimal, or even an increment in the figure before the point in the case of the euro (or in relation to the former US dollar/Deutschmark price), can generate real changes in the mood of market participants. Although, for instance, a downwards movement from $1.0999 to $1.1000 represents a rise of only $0.0001 per euro, it can cause a bullish mood as the first part of the number is perceived more clearly than the rest of the digits $**1.09**99 and $**1.10**00. This increment represents a totally different situation, due to the anchoring to the initial digits. The euro is suddenly much steadier.

Never place a market order for a "round" figure or at a "psychological level". This will set you up for trouble, as everyone wants to trade at this level and you can therefore expect high activity. In the case of stop loss orders in particular, you must expect execution at worse prices.

Risks inherent in representativity

Representativity plays an important role in the estimation of probability, which traders must decide on immediately before decisions.

The question often arises in trading as to how high the probability is that an event will occur, based on the similarity to the elements of a certain class of news. Examples of the three variants of representativity can, of course, also be found in the financial markets. False conclusions, which are based on an overvaluation of probability, play a large role – especially when there is time pressure.

The larger the quantity of information in certain situations, the stronger the trust in one's own judgment, even if the information is old or partly irrelevant. In particular, when information is interrelated and matches, then one's own perception is often overvalued, causing people and events to be judged wrongly (Kahneman and Tversky 1973).

Play devil's advocate if complex information appears plausible and reliable. Pretend to not believe the information. Prove it wrong.

Many market participants tend to order analyses from economically oriented divisions of several banks at the same time when shares or currency prices are concerned. When two or three of these calculations show similar results based on the same arguments or similar ones, then the other predictions are generally discarded, even though the participants may realize that similar analyses may well be based on the same data, or that the authors know each other and have mutually compared their opinions. This can have fatal consequences if the underlying material was not researched well or was subject to errors.

Similar analyses from several sources increase the confidence that the forecast is right. Assume that opinions have usually been compared. A stock that is recommended ten times over is not necessarily ten times as good as stock that is recommended only once.

The second variant of an overvaluation of probability, the "gambler's fallacy", is also encountered in trading rooms. A currency or share that has been showing a clear rise at close of trade for 11 consecutive days is not popular. "What goes up must go down," goes the saying on the stock exchange. But even if each individual price rise was purely coincidental, this does not mean that after 11 positive days the twelfth will be negative. We should certainly not assume "compensatory" justice if there is a causal relationship (and thus predictability) between the individual price movements (e.g. a trend).

Don't let yourself be reassured. What goes up may well continue to rise. What is cheap today may be even cheaper tomorrow. Trends are generally created because at the start nobody believes in them.

A further aspect of representativity and the possible overvaluation of causal relationships are trends and fashions. Clothes become fashionable when they are worn by famous people who are looked up to. A single important personality can often start a new trend or fashion on his own. These fashions soon gain a large number of followers, particularly when such fashions also prove to be profitable. Remember the gold digger mood in the Wild West, or the pyramid businesses that continue to appear in droves? Even though it is well known that only the original players earn money from them, highly intelligent people still continue to take part in them.

Remember that the golden egg is only worth something when only you own it. If the majority of market participants expresses a unanimous opinion, then they will normally not find enough opponents to realize the resulting profits.

Currency markets are also subject to certain fashions. The interest of actors continues to focus on a particular statistic amongst the mass of published data, particularly with regard to economic data. US data nearly always receive more attention amongst market participants in the case of the euro/US dollar ratio. The attention was focused on the US money supply statistics in the early 1980s, for example. The emphasis later changed to gross national product figures. The consumer price or manufacturers' price index played an important role at times when the interest rate was subjected to large changes. Suddenly, the focus changed to balance of trade figures, and in recent years job market data became increasingly popular. All these data are ultimately regarded as particularly representative for the US economy.

Or take an expert who is regarded as successful by the majority of market participants. When the expert finally decides on a certain forecasting method and finds it useful, then this method will also be adopted by the actors, even if it is controversial. Only the current success of the expert counts for them, and therefore the instruments he uses are also considered to be useful. Once the method of forecasting is generally recognized, acceptance will be even greater based on this "confirmation". Predictions offer the illusion of being able to control the market. And the more logical they appear to be, the more people think it probable that they will come true. People are reassured and believe they can make sound decisions.

Do not trust an individual "recognized" professional revered by many actors as a guru. Remember: you will be in the same boat as everybody else if he gets it wrong. Should the boat go under, then there is a risk of collective loss of control, characterized by panic. Collect opinions and judgments from other analysts as well.

Now consider the analyst who suddenly becomes the center of attention, for even a few consecutive successful forecasts are sufficient to give an analyst the seal of approval. His skills are, however, generally overvalued. Analysts have become stars after entering the limelight with six consecutive successful forecasts under their belt (i.e. a 100 per cent hit rate) although they never stood out before. Only by using a certain time window – their short-term success soon gets known – do such previously unknown people become famous. The disappointment will be greater if subsequent predictions do not keep their promise and the star falls again.

Similarly, a trend may be read prematurely into a small number of positive economic data in the field of fundamental analysis, even though the small quantity of data does not justify such a con-clusion. Future movements of a currency will, for example, be decided on the basis of a impressively depicted graphical representation of important fundamental data. It is possible that this is based on much too short a time window and on four or five positive examples that seem representative but may well have arisen by chance. If you look long enough, then you will find many indices for statistical relationships in time series.

The assimilation and processing of information is subject to systematic distortions. Nevertheless, information is the main factor influencing actual decisions in favor of or against a trade by traders and all other market participants, whether professional or amateur. Information increases the sense of being in control of the future. It is clear that we cannot assume that most actors assimilate and process information in the same way, even if it is comprehensive and freely available.

OPEN POSITIONS: SMALL GAINS AND LARGE LOSSES

To be or not to be? Hamlet's question of destiny does not apply to all market participants about to make a decision. Yet to make a decision means wanting to change the present situation. Players in the financial markets are, in the first instance, interested in a change in their economic situation, either because they wish to protect themselves against unforeseen developments, or to profit from market developments. Each trading decision – whether resulting in a transaction or not – is made on the basis of a selection from alternatives. There are therefore at least two possibilities. People decide in favor of one alternative in order to realize its advantages and to avoid the disadvantages of the other choices. The market participant can soon feel overtaxed if the choices are of a complex nature. People may not weigh up properly all the possibilities if a decision includes many, possibly multilevel, choices; they may thus be tempted to make an impulsive choice. When players are compelled to make such a decision – for instance, due to external restrictions such as loss limits – they may avoid a decision and embark upon a flight strategy (Mann 1994) that is not necessarily rational but entails a postponement.

The objective of each decision is realization and control of the future. This would be relatively unproblematic if decisions could be made under conditions of certainty, yet 100 per cent certainty does not exist. Nobody can grasp all the consequences of a decision, and so success remains uncertain. People therefore fall back on forecasts – either their own or those compiled by others – in order to avoid making a wrong decision. This, in turn, requires information that must be perceived correctly and processed logically; traders are not always successful in doing this, as we saw earlier.

As decisions (insofar as they lead to a transaction in the markets) affect the current market price in the form of additional demand and supply, they play a key role in future price movements and therefore also in respect of new forecasts generated by analysts. But postponed decisions may also affect the future development of market prices, because they may have to be made at a later stage.

Determine a price target and a stop loss before each trade. Make sure that the target profit is approximately three times as large as the amount that you are prepared to risk.[2] Don't set the stop loss too low: give the market some space to breathe.

Those who mingle daily with traders will be able to observe the classical errors of realizing profits quickly (and too soon) and not stopping losses in time hundreds of times a day. Let us look at the situation of a short-term currency trader before he takes a position. He faces a choice that is similar to the one faced by subjects in the bets and lottery examples given in this book. The term "lottery" in this context does not imply that traders are of the same nature as gamblers; rather, the term represents a generalization of situations in which a decision maker, who is not influenced by additional information, acts. The result of his actions is – as in a win on the lottery – measurable in monetary terms. Market

[2] We will dispense with a detailed explanation of this rule, which has been proven in practice. When you start with a possible price rise of 150 euros for a share, for example, you can risk one third, i.e. the difference between your stop loss and the cash price must not be more than 50 euros.

participants, in contrast to lottery players, do not know the exact probability of a future win or loss. They must decide under a condition of considerable uncertainty. They may be disadvantaged compared with lottery players, who run risks that can be measured. They must nevertheless arrive at an exact idea of what it is they are prepared to risk.

Strictly speaking, there is a third alternative to the choices of "buy" or "sell": doing nothing. This is usually the case when an actor cannot form a clear idea of the market process. Either he cannot judge opportunities and risks, or he believes that he does not have sufficient information. Doing nothing also means earning nothing in the case of a trader, therefore not realizing his objective in certain circumstances.

In addition, we must distinguish between a trader taking a position voluntarily and being more or less pushed into a trade by a third party. The latter is the case when a bank has to quote a price to one of its customers or even a competitor, which is then traded. In this case, the trader normally does not have much time to consider the matter, in contrast to a situation requiring a voluntary decision. If he can liquidate the undesired position with a profit, albeit a very small one (often even at par), then he will do this immediately, especially when trading large volumes. He assumes that the counterparty possibly has more to place, and this could affect the price.

Often, the trader fears – depending on how important the counterparty is – that his opponent is in possession of relevant information and could take advantage of this knowledge. If he can liquidate the position he was forced to take only at a loss, then he will normally sit out the position, at least for a while. Most traders therefore tend to act risk-averse in the profit zone and to take risks in the loss zone. Losses are only realized immediately when the counterparty is thought to have a strong market position, such as the central bank. Traders will then try to neutralize their losses by taking the same position as their counterparty, i.e. they hitch a ride in the hope that the other side is strong enough to influence the market price further in the direction it has now taken. But now we are dealing with a decision that is surrounded by many individual imponderables, as it is normally only based on the assumption that the trading partner is strong enough to initiate a movement. The immense time pressure on such actions – decisions must often be made in seconds – leads to the fact that the trading alternatives and their consequences are ill-considered, i.e. they are compared and executed only on instinct.

In order to clear a position one is forced to take without incurring a loss, currency prices are quoted with spreads (i.e. with a bid and offer price). There is no guarantee that the trader will actually earn this spread; it serves only as protection, as it is not known how the counterparty will respond. These spreads have shrunk considerably of late in the currency markets, due to sharp competition in the liquid markets, so traders should be pleased if they still manage to make a profit. Greater spreads can now only be found in less liquid markets – the risk of finding sufficient partners here for liquidating positions is considerably greater.

A short-term trader is in a slightly better position, as he is free to decide whether and when he will enter a position. He should have a relatively clear idea of the probability and magnitude of a rise or a fall in the price of, say, the euro. He will indicate reasonably confidently a figure between 70 and 80 per cent if asked about the probability that the intended profit will be realized, a figure that is, however, completely subjective in contrast to a bet with a fixed probability. His estimate will normally be too high, due to the tendency to overvalue one's own skills.

Yet he will often produce hit rates at around 80 per cent. The real reason, however, is that gains are realized much too early compared with losses. High hit rates are not surprising when paper gains are normally realized after a price movement of no more than 0.5 per cent, while one is willing to let losses grow to three per cent. A movement of 0.5 per cent in the price of a currency occurs much more often than a three per cent change in a direction.

Remember that a high hit rate for your transactions does not guarantee high profits.

Surprisingly, many traders do not have a concrete idea of how high a profit they are aiming for before entering into a commitment. Often, medium-term and generally technically oriented analyses are used for short-term trades, usually in the (mostly illusory) hope that their short-term targets will be reached quickly, possibly even within two to three hours.

Like the participants in one of the bets described earlier, short-term traders also have a reference point before entering a position, namely the amount they must earn in a certain period of time. Actors will have reached their goals once they have realized this objective; they then have a balanced account. The reference point for their performance will be exactly at the point of the kink in the value curve (Figure 7-1). Traders will therefore mentally be "in the red" at the start of the trading period.

If the target is to earn, say, two million euros per annum, then he will mentally start in the loss area of the value function with a balance of minus two million euros, although the real starting point of the performance at the start of the period under consideration (e.g. the start of the year, month or day) is actually at zero. The objective of achieving a profit target therefore also causes a shift in the reference point.

Nevertheless, especially at the start of the month or year, many traders do not like to start with a loss, most preferring to start with

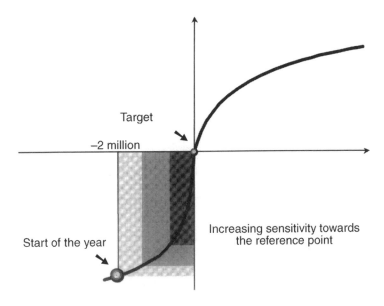

Figure 7-1 Hypothetical value function with a performance target of two million euros. Note that the profit target becomes the reference point.

small volumes. Trading decisions may also be prepared with more care at the beginning. Traders try to form a proper picture of the market and to follow the advice of a third party, and at first they will only enter a position if they are quite sure of things. They buy, for instance, ten million euros at price x, equalling $1.0800, for analyses predict that the euro will soon rise to $1.2000. The total performance sinks into the background in the subconscious of the actors at the same time as the position is opened: a new reference point, the cash price of the position, replaces the original reference point. Mentally, a new account will be opened.

Keep your trading volume as constant as possible. Be as courageous in January as in July. The trading volume must on no account be increased on the basis of a series of successes, nor should it be reduced by a large amount after a negative series.

The cash price of a position determines success or failure; it represents the difference between grudging recognition and patronizing pity on the part of colleagues. It will influence the future behavior of the actor just as much as the subjects in the experiments, who had to choose between a certain gain and the chance of a gain at a certain probability (or make a decision between a certain loss and a particular risk).

Behavior when making a profit

Assuming the price of the euro rises by $0.0050, a relatively small amount, then the trader will wonder whether he ought to realize this paper profit or not, even if he originally perhaps had his eye on a price rise of two cents. He has a choice between a certain profit of $ 0.0050 per euro, i.e. $50,000 at ten million euros, if he clears the position, or a chance to earn a total of $0.0200 per euro (resulting in a $200,000 profit if the price target is realized) weighted with a probability; however, this also includes the risk of possibly losing everything again.

The second alternative may present a problem for the trader insofar that he may have to estimate the probability of the target

price being reached again (unlike the lottery, where this probability is fixed from the start) on the basis of new information, and
may also have to review the reasons in favor of the original
position. In most cases, there will be little time to think it over, as
prices can change very quickly. Most actors will decide in favor of
the certain profit, not only because of the emotional state of joy but
also because of a changed and considerably simplified risk perception. There is a chance that the price will continue to rise and
will reach the decision maker's target price of $0.0200, but this will
be estimated to be less likely than the risk that the price will fall
again by $0.0050 to the cash price (the reference point) so that the
paper profit will be wiped out. The cash price is, in fact, nearer than
the target price in the actor's view (Figure 7-2).

The time factor plays a very important role. If a position is in the
profit area, then time is certainly seen as a threat: paper profits
may melt away while waiting, while any still uncertain profit is

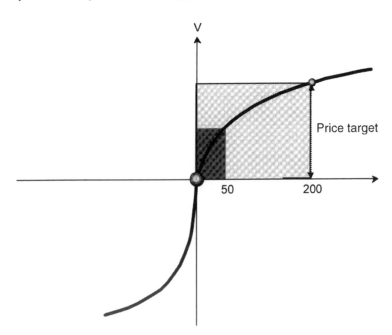

Figure 7-2   Trader's hypothetical function. The position is in the profit zone.
Considering the value for the first 50 points of profit, projected on ordinate v, we
can see that the remaining (only probable) 150 points do not weigh much more,
due to decreasing sensitivity.

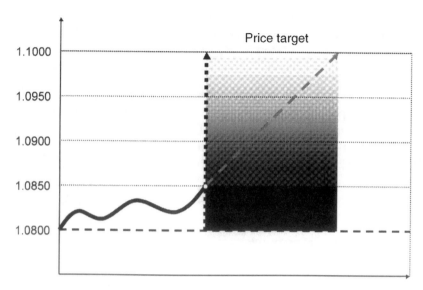

Figure 7-3   A different view of the position shown in Figure 7-2. The position, purchased at a price of $1.0800 in the profit zone with 50 points after a certain time period, equals a certain profit of $50,000 upon liquidation.

additionally discounted due to future uncertainty. People become impatient. We may therefore assume that a short-term target originally chosen by the actor will be continuously pulled in towards the current market price level (Figure 7-3).

In our experience, when traders have to evaluate the probability of the risk that the price will return to the cash price, they will estimate the probability as considerably higher than 50 per cent, therefore the probability of the originally planned profit target being realized is considerably lower than 50 per cent, especially if the position was opened some time ago, which may have reduced the confidence of the actors. They tend to think that it is still a long way to the price target (more precisely, three times as far as back to the cash price). A thorough review of the probability – for instance, using the results of further analyses – is generally omitted. The hope to earn, for instance, $50,000 more is less great, due to decreasing sensitivity, than the fear of losing the paper profit of $50,000 again. People are aware of the risks, so they act risk-averse (Figure 7-4).

Never liquidate a position because you are losing patience or becoming increasingly fearful while waiting for a profit.

The situation is psychologically rather more favorable if the trader has let the paper profit run a little further, say to $0.0080, which would amount to $80,000 at ten million euros. In this case, it is only $0.0120 to the price target originally chosen. Nevertheless, even here the risk of a fall is perceived as greater than the chance that the price target will actually be reached, as the present price is still closer to the cash price (reference point) of the position than to the target price.

If you are tempted to realize profits before reaching your originally chosen price target, imagine that you had entered the opposite position. You would then have suffered a loss instead of a profit on paper. Would you want to realize this loss?

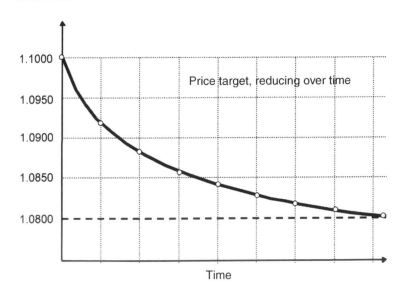

Figure 7-4 Hypothetical position with the cash price at $1.0800. The target price (bold line) was set at $1.1000. Over time, particularly at the start of trading, there is a strong tendency to increasingly rein in the target, so that the trader is even prepared to liquidate the position at par in the end.

The risk of premature profit taking will be reduced significantly only when more than half – $0.0100 in our example – of the price potential originally hoped for has been reached, as the distance from the current price to the reference point of the cash price is initially greater than the distance to the target price. The risk of a fall will then intuitively be estimated as smaller than the chance of the full profit: hope will weigh more than fear. Even so, the inclination to realize paper profits remains.

If the trader did not pin himself down to a target price when entering the position, then the inclination to take profits prematurely will still be present, as only the risk of a fall in the price will ever be compared to realization of the profit, and additional profits do not count as much as the fear of having to relinquish what has already been achieved, based on decreasing sensitivity.

Behavior in the case of a loss

The situation is different when faced with a loss. Imagine that the euro falls by $0.0050 below the purchase price of $1.0800. The trader again has a choice between an alternative with a certain outcome (liquidating the position) and an event with an uncertain outcome. He must decide between a certain loss of $0.0050 per euro, which is a deficit of $50,000 at ten million euros if the position is liquidated, and the chance of possibly losing nothing, linked to the risk of going even further into the red, weighted with a probability that is still to be estimated.

But perhaps the trader risks reaching his daily reportable limit, when he must notify his boss immediately, if he waits any longer. On the profit side, there is no such duty to inform the boss; large losses must, on the other hand, always be reported. Such limits, which people may also set themselves, are often also the point at which the position must be liquidated in any case.

Set yourself a stop loss before entering the transaction, and then do not exceed this under any circumstances.

Assuming such a limit is $200,000 ($0.02 at ten million euros[3]), this means that the trader with a cash price of $1.0800 would have to respond no later than at a spot price of $1.0600. The risk of the second alternative therefore becomes quantifiable, at least as far as value is concerned; the probability that this will occur can only be estimated subjectively as before. The trader therefore has a choice of realizing a loss of $50,000 on the one hand, and the chance of making up the loss, linked to a high risk of losing $200,000 should the worst happen. Should there, on the other hand, be no loss limit or reportable limit (this applies particularly to all market participants acting on their own behalf), then there is a risk that losses could quickly move to a level considerably higher than was foreseen at the start (Figure 7-5).

The possibility that the opening price is reached again will be estimated intuitively as considerably higher than the risk to actually have to realize a loss of $200,000. After all, the movement of $0.0050 in the direction of the cash price (reference point) seems easier to trace back than a stretch of a further (uncertain) $0.0150 in the wrong direction. And time is also a factor – this time as a useful one, as only time renders it possible that market participants will be able to make up for paper losses. Waiting might pay off, while the still uncertain losses are played down as a possible risk, which in addition lies in the distant future. People are patient – as long as there is hope of reaching the purchase price again. The trader will indicate the probability of a favorable outcome at a minimum of 50 per cent, in accordance with his own logic; the risk of a complete loss is therefore estimated at a maximum of 50 per cent. However, he will actually consider this probability to be less, due to a healthy amount of confidence (in particular, when the accumulated loss has arisen only slowly). There were, after all, any number of sound reasons for entering the position, and he normally has a high hit rate.

Don't waste time on unprofitable positions. Remember that this will lock up your money, which you then cannot use for other, more profitable transactions.

---

[3] Note that the amount of $0.02 has been chosen for reasons of comparability in relation to the profit side; these limits could well be set differently in reality.

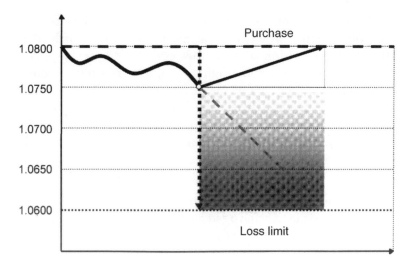

Figure 7-5 Position with a cash price of $1.0800, which has slid into the loss zone by 0.0050 points. The distance to the cash price will be perceived as less than the possible risk of reaching the loss limit.

Most traders are reluctant to settle for a certain loss, just like the subjects in the experiment described in Chapter 4. Losses are not realized, as most people cling to the principle of hope and firmly believe that everything will be all right in the end. The majority proves to be only too willing to take risks below the cash price. This has been confirmed by more recent experiments amongst currency dealers; in a comparable situation, more than 70 per cent of those questioned showed such behavior (Oberlechner and Hocking, 1997).

It is therefore understandable in such a situation that the actor wishes to reduce the gap between the cash price and the spot price in order to strengthen his belief that he will be able to liquidate his position without incurring a loss. He will be able to achieve this objective if he buys euros in addition to his existing position ("mixing"). In this way, he can also reduce the dissonance experienced in response to the paper loss (putting up with an increased commitment). Should he, for instance, double his position from ten to 20 million euros, then the gap between the spot price and the purchase price would be reduced by half. Should the trader buy a further ten million euros at, say, $1.0700, then the purchase price would improve from the original $1.0800 to $1.0750. The loss limit, on the other hand, would be reached after $0.01 (which makes $200,000 at 20 million euros); this corresponds to a price of $1.0650 instead of $1.0600 (Figure 7-6). The reference point of the cash price is then just as far removed as before in respect of the loss limit. The surprising thing is that most traders would be happy to reach the cash price again in such a situation, in which case they would clear the position immediately. The fact that they are actually back to where they started seems to matter little to them.

Don't increase your position by additional mixing of further positions once you have entered the loss zone. Your opening price will only be improved through averaging, while your trade volume on the other hand increases considerably. ·   ·

Decreasing sensitivity confirms the tendency on the part of the trader to let losses run, as the effect causes additional losses (which could occur by leaving the position open) to be perceived less

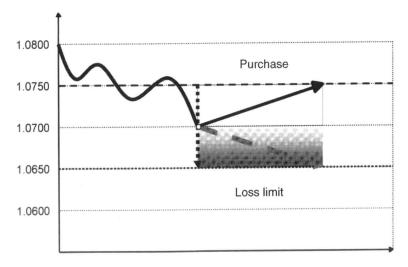

Figure 7-6   The cash price of $1.0800 will be improved to $1.0750 by buying a further ten million euros at a price of $1.0700. This also reduces the loss limit from $1.0600 to $1.0650.

strongly than possible price rises (which relate to the purchase price) (Figure 7-7). This behavior is denoted by the sunk cost effect. Increasing a "wrong" position through additional mixing does not make the position better in the end: it only appears better because the spot price moves closer to the (new) purchase price (Figure 7-8).

The tendency to let loss positions run does not change when the spot price is closer to the loss limit than to the purchase price. Additional losses will still be valued less than the regained ground.

Risk taking only disappears when the loss has reached a magnitude very close to the reportable loss limit. People would, in any case, avoid this as unauthorized exceeding of this limit normally invokes sanctions, which could cause the value function to end up in a zone comparable to the one shown in Chapter 4.

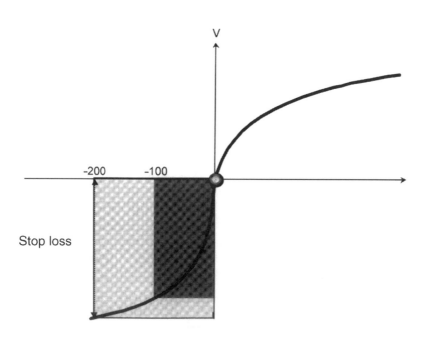

Figure 7-7 Hypothetical value function. The price is in the loss zone with 100 points ($0.0100). A loss of a further 100 points would be perceived with decreasing sensitivity, as the light-colored hatching shows.

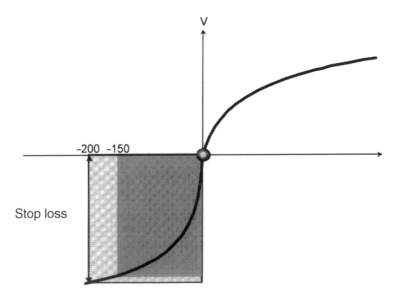

Figure 7-8   Hypothetical value function showing that the last 50 points (light hatching) do not matter very much.

Behavior following liquidation and the influence of the performance on future risk behavior

The cash price loses its importance with the complete liquidation of the position – it no longer exists, and the mental account "euro/dollar position" is closed. In its place, the original reference point, the total performance of the trader, comes into focus again. The new gain or loss must be posted to the mental account "performance", to which all individual gains and losses are posted.

In common with all mental accounts, this one is also subject to typical laws, as the value function that is kinked at the reference point shows, i.e. losses count heavier than similar-sized gains, and the further they are removed from the reference point, the less they are perceived. The balance of this account therefore has a real effect on the future risk-taking or risk-averse behavior of the trader and on the size of subsequent positions.

Choose a position size that you can sustain through longish periods of drought (sustained losses) without becoming overapprehensive.

If the account "performance" is situated in the profit zone, then the trader will be inclined to reduce his risks; he will therefore behave risk-averse. Additional gains will no longer be experienced as strongly, the size of the position remaining equal. If the account shows a loss, then the actor will increase his risks as he pays more attention to losses made good (up to the reference point) but no longer experiences additional losses that are as bad, due to decreasing sensitivity.

Even if it is difficult, keep your position volumes constant. Do not increase your activities just because you have been particularly successful recently.

As mentioned earlier, the reference point of the "performance" account does not equal zero for most traders; rather, it is equal to the profit target set by his employer (in this case a bank). The trader will therefore still be in the loss zone, even after his first successful trade, unless the first profit of the period under consideration immediately covers the budget. It is therefore not surprising that people continue to take risks: a series of small but successfully concluded positions would clearly affect confidence, and as a result the size of the positions. Recall the greed of the currency trader introduced in Chapter 2, which often rears its head in this situation, as well as the desire to fulfill the profit target as quickly as possible.

The trader will normally no longer take risks but will act risk-averse due to the now decreased sensitivity, once the reference point "budget" (situated at the origin of the hypothetical value function) has been reached. He will therefore tend to reduce his future positions. He will no longer perceive additional gains as intensively as before, as his performance is now situated in the positive zone of the value function. Should the performance slide below the reference point, however, then this would be experienced considerably more strongly than an increase of a similar amount on the profit side.

A survey of currency traders showed an additional effect: it was found that risk taking amongst most traders clearly decreases after a series of losses (Oberlechner and Hocking 1997). This can be explained easily. A strong control deficit kicks in in the case of several consecutive losses: the actor recognizes that he is less in control of the situation than he assumed himself to be. On the other hand, we must not forget that the loss limits of most traders are defined relatively strictly. Although they will perceive a rising number of losses in the negative zone with decreasing sensitivity, from a certain magnitude onwards extreme loss aversion will take over due to the looming limit, which can be compared to the bankruptcy of a company or to the cessation of all trading activities (see also Chapter 4). They must not exceed these loss limits under any circumstances, so they avoid the risk in advance by drastically reducing their positions (Figure 7-9).

Remember that experience shows that when you reduce the size of your positions after a series of losses, you will redeem your negative balance only after a long period of time. This task can be difficult and frustrating.

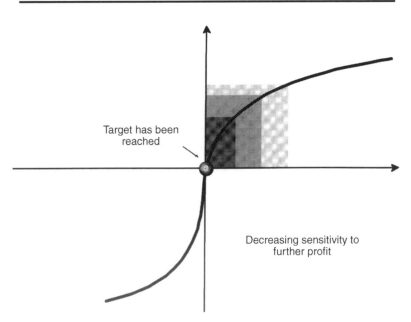

Figure 7-9   Hypothetical value function. The budget has been achieved. The gray areas represent possible increases in performance above the profit target. Each gray step marks an additional profit, which is perceived with decreasing sensitivity and therefore leads to risk aversion.

The tendency to increase positions after a series of successes, or to reduce them following a series of losses, has a significant effect on the success of a market participant, in particular when he is used to high hit rates due to premature profit taking and a loss limit that is too generous (Figure 7-10). This may mean that the trader will increase his trading volume after a short series of small profits. Any subsequent losses with an increased position will not only obliviate the previous gains but will soon lead to a considerable overall loss. A few unlucky transactions will increase the overall loss to the extent that the loss limit laid down by the management looms threateningly. Traders then decide (or a supervisor fearing the worst will tell them) to enter only very small trading volumes from then on, which may amount to only one-quarter of the position size originally chosen. It will be a miracle if the negative performance can be made up at this rate.

The profit targets set by the management are therefore extremely significant. If the performance target is reached very quickly, perhaps because it was set too low, then the trader arrives

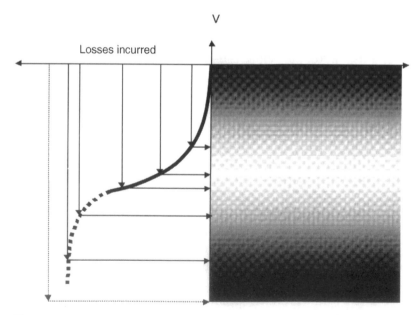

Figure 7-10   Hypothetical value function as an example of a profit target at the start of the year. The darker the field, the stronger the perception of gain in the vicinity of the profit target, or of loss in the vicinity of the limit.

too soon in the positive zone of the value function and his behavior will be too restrained. Why should he run unnecessary risks when he has reached his target and even received a bonus for this? Moreover, nobody asked whether he could achieve even more when the target was reached. A trader will therefore try to avoid a result that is "too good", because this will serve as a new future target or reference point. On the other hand, when profit targets are set too high, then this may have a demotivating effect due to the downwards curve of the value function in the negative zone in certain circumstances. People are sometimes willing to run disproportionately high risks, even early on in the trading period, in order to leave this sector as quickly as possible.

The behavior of medium- and long-term market participants

Decreasing sensitivity, loss aversion and dependency on a reference point also apply to market participants with medium-term horizons. They have the same reference points for measuring success as market participants who trade short term. They are also subject to the disposition effect and will realize their profits too early or leave losses to run for too long. The absolute size of the gains and losses is usually greater, but the ratio of gains to losses is the same.

Take a commercial, medium-term participant in the currency market who has a choice between taking out insurance against future price movements by hedging or sitting it out, if he has an invoice or a delivery in a foreign currency. This means that an exporter will enter a position when he issues an invoice, while an importer will do so when confirming an order in a foreign currency. His decision to hedge against future currency fluctuations is similar to evening up his position, the purchase price being equal to the exchange rate used for the invoice or order. The same purchase price is also the reference point if the actor does not hedge his commitment immediately after issuing the invoice or order confirmation in a foreign currency. He will therefore not run a currency risk. However, the slightest delay between the moment the currency risk is known and evening up – as little as one minute – leads to the known reference point phenomenon.

Say an exporter in Europe signs an agreement to supply goods to a value of five million dollars to the USA, based on an exchange rate of $1.1000 per euro. Regardless of whether this exchange rate is realistic, it will play an important role as a future reference point if the currency risk is not hedged immediately. Should the dollar in the meantime move above the calculated price (due to an unintended or deliberate delay following the signing of the contract), then the inclination will be to realize the profit (prematurely). Such sums, which have arisen incidentally, are often seen as windfall profits, for the exporter actually intended to hedge the currency risk. It would therefore be sensible on the part of the exporter to behave risk-averse in such a situation. The exporter is likely to take more risks if the price of the dollar moves below the calculated price, in the hope of making up the loss. Something similar applies to the importer, who must hedge a commitment.

Do not look upon incidentally generated windfall profits as an exceptional profit to be treated carelessly. Remember that there may be incidental losses also, which are not so easy to make up.

Currency dealers are often given calculation prices (especially by merchants) that are dictated by a third party, e.g. by a firm or the purchasing department. It often turns out that the prices underlying the calculation do not, or no longer, correspond to market conditions. Perhaps the partner was abroad, but they wanted to conclude the transaction at any price.

Often, calculation prices are laid down for a relatively long period (e.g. three months) in advance, irrespective of how the market subsequently develops. The currency manager will be inclined to hedge most positions quickly if such a price has been calculated too much in his favor, i.e. if he finds himself above his reference point. Should the calculation turn out to be unfavorable for the trader, then he will tend to leave the losses to run, as he is below the reference point. Calculation prices that are unfavorable for the currency trader can, on the other hand, mean a competitive advantage for the purchasing or sales department of a company.

It is questionable, however, whether the profits made in this way will be sufficient to offset the losses that may arise when the currency department is not sufficiently disciplined.

Similarly, loss aversion, and in particular mental accounting, plays an important role in firms in which the currency division is required to make a contribution to profits independently from the core business, as there is a change of reference point between the "performance" account and the separate mental evaluation of the individual "position" accounts in the case of the short-term actor.

This also applies to investors and asset management firms that deal, for example, in foreign securities and therefore also run a currency risk. The reference point is formed by the price at which the foreign shares, bonds etc. have been bought. Note that a separate mental account, "currency", is opened when buying the securities.

Do not underestimate any possible foreign currency risk accompanying trading in foreign securities. Treat the former with the same care as your actual transaction.

Note that a meaningful, early loss limitation (e.g. a stop loss procedure) is often not possible in the case of asset management firms, however strict the discipline may be, as the scale of the transactions does not allow for a quick response without further loss. Often, markets are not capable of absorbing such high volumes without large price repercussions. As a result, prices slide, even during the transaction. On the other hand, there is the advantage on the profit side that large positions can be liquidated carefully and gradually, even when one is inclined to premature profit taking.

Some dependency on reference points is also evident in the behavior of long-term private investors, for the purchase price is never quite forgotten. Even when yields from assets serve only to keep the capital intact despite inflation, there will still be an intention to make a profit. And although the pressure of having to make an immediate profit is considerably less than for a professional trader, a private position in shares or fixed-interest bonds also has a reference point, with obvious consequences. But purchase prices in the case of such generally long-term positions are often simply forgotten if the invested capital serves, for instance, as a nest egg or is left for descendants to inherit. The purchase price is irrelevant in the case of an inheritance, and even when losses have been made on paper, the inheritors will not have a problem with liquidating the position.

BET ON THE WRONG HORSE? – MIXED FEELINGS AFTER A DECISION

People often feel that not everything went as well as it could have after a trading decision, be it opening or liquidating a position. Cognitive dissonance (see Chapter 5) may arise, especially in the case of loss-making trades. A precondition for the generation of dissonance is that a decision maker has made a provisional choice between at least two alternative actions, and must have committed himself to a certain extent. This is typically the case for individual positions (one enters a position) in the financial markets. It is different, of course, if players are only acting on behalf of a third party or are forced into a transaction (e.g. by a supervisor). For instance, if a supervisor has dictated the liquidation without the trader having been party to the decision.

Dissonance can be reduced in two ways. Either the decision is reviewed, or the attitude created by the prior decision is "corrected" (by collecting additional information or putting a different interpretation on particular information) and adapted to reality.

Reducing dissonance by revising the trading decision

Participants in the financial markets are confronted daily with the question as to whether they should liquidate an existing trade or not. In particular, open positions that are accumulating a paper loss will generate doubt and inner conflict (dissonant cognition). But profits may also give rise to mixed feelings – for instance, when one has decided on a currency trade in US dollars, and a different position (for instance British pounds) would have turned out considerably better. Or when an even higher profit would have been possible with a position, had the timing been better.

Always concentrate on exposures that are open at the time. Ignore "had", "could" and "would".

In most cases (if the market is not closed or illiquid), it is possible to reverse a decision surrounded by doubt and regret by liquidating the trade. The extent of psychological resistance against this step depends on the size of the material loss, as well as on the strength of the psychological discomfort, which realization of the loss could invoke. For the player suffers loss of face, particularly when his decision is observed by many other market participants, and his reputation suffers if he is obviously a "loser".

This method of reducing dissonance is therefore usually avoided, particularly as it brings with it the risk of fresh dissonance. Such might be the case if the trade was liquidated at a bad time and prices subsequently moved again in the direction originally hoped for. This means that a consonant cognition – hope – accompanies each open position with a paper loss, as long as there is still a possibility of prices developing in the right direction: realizing the loss would thus entail relinquishing the optimistic emotion. This applies particularly at the start of a trade, when such a loss is still relatively small, for the hope that this possible loss may be neutralized in time is, at this stage, still relatively great. Any loss created upon liquidation of the position would be heavier than the associated elimination of dissonant cognition.

Do not refer to the cash price when faced with the dilemma of liquidating a trade or continuing to let it run. Do not base this decision on the outcome of earlier transactions.

When players are in the profit zone, they experience this as consonant. There is no reason to worry. But the risk of losing the profit just made through a reversal of the price movement is always present. We know that annoyance in relation to a profit lost is greater than the joy experienced when the profit first arose. All market participants would prefer to avoid this unpleasant state, and indeed they try to avoid this: in short, they liquidate their position as a wise precaution. Note that this fits in with the typical behavior of most players to prefer a certain gain to a potential higher gain.

Do not let yourself be rattled by corrective movements that go against you when you are in the profit zone. Corrections are necessarily present in sound trends; they should not tempt you into premature profit taking.

Any price developments that continue unexpectedly following liquidation of the position could also give rise to dissonance. A precondition is, however, that the person in question continues to follow the market after closing his position, i.e. he must be aware of the profit foregone. The dissonance can, in this case, be eliminated quite quickly in theory simply by turning one's back on the market and opening a new position. Unfortunately, most actors act much too quickly, and important information (e.g. warnings) are overlooked in their haste and determination not to miss out.

Do not return to the market so as not to miss out. Forget the last transaction if you cannot leave well alone. Now would you still enter a new trade?

Reducing dissonance by selecting and reinterpreting particular information

The reduction in dissonance brought about by changing the cognitions involved is easier for most market participants than changing a decision once made. A reduction in the dissonance may be achieved by reducing the weight or significance of the dissonant cognitions. This could be quite difficult in the case of a paper loss that a market participant has suffered as a result of his trading decision. One can't play around with the actual size of the loss, unless one has deliberately miscalculated. Many will, for instance, try to play down the loss sustained. This could be done in this case through the addition of a consonant cognition for instance, possibly by recalling a positive memory. This behavior is seen in many actors, in particular when losses are not yet excessive. If, on the other hand, the loss is somewhat higher, then it might be harder to ignore. But there is still the hope that everything will turn out OK, which may reduce dissonance in the decision maker.

Another opportunity for reducing dissonance is offered by mental accounting. Gains and losses are offset or compared with each other, e.g. a loss on the euro can be offset against gains in the British pound, the yen and the franc. Even if the performance ultimately stays at zero, people will tell themselves that they are successful, for each of the profits will be experienced individually and therefore the success in total will be experienced more strongly than the single loss – a classic case of glossing things over.

Reducing dissonance by adding positive cognition occurs in market participants who are in a loss situation, and through the confirmation they seek from third parties that the original decision was the right one. This is particularly necessary when the decision maker does not have sufficient consonant cognitions available. At the same time, the consonant reasons as to why the trading decision was made in the first place are looked at once more. If this attitude is not confirmed by others, and if the absence of confirmation is perceived as negative, particularly if their own opinion is rejected by others, then this would equal an addition of dissonant cognitions. Mixing with people who are of a different opinion is therefore avoided as much as possible, and if unsuccessful, people will try to play down any criticisms or contrary opinions, or even disparage these.

Do not use the opinion of others to justify trades in the loss zone, or to make them appear better than they are.

People may be particularly aggressive towards an analyst according to whose forecast the player would sustain further losses, or they may question their professional abilities. On the other hand, an "expert" with a reputation of being unsuccessful may acquire unexpected fame when his predictions are perceived as consonant by a decision maker. Even if the forecasts are not logically consistent, the existence of such predictions is sufficient and the status of the analyst will be enhanced – he may even be praised.

Do not be guided by the fact that you are told what you want to hear when choosing your analyst. Look for one who compiles sharp analyses, even when these may not always suit you.

The search for additional consonant cognition has an effect on the perception of new information in particular. News that has a dissonance-reducing effect will be preferred to that which increases dissonance, i.e. information is perceived increasingly selectively. As a result, only information that is judged as supporting the position, according to the logic of the decision maker, will be sought out. Whether this information is of an economic or market-related nature is irrelevant. Even information that normally is not relevant to developments in the market can suddenly become important. Market information that does not support the decision made originally will, on the other hand, be "bent" or glossed over if it cannot be ignored completely. This opens the floodgates for the distorted perception of information, as well as its assimilation.

The selective quest for consonant information can have a dramatic effect when the actor finds himself in the same situation as other market participants. Such a situation could, for instance, occur in a trading firm when several traders have entered a similar trade. Imagine that a rise in interest rates is expected in the USA, and therefore dollars have been bought against several other currencies. In the meantime, the US currency has unexpectedly come under pressure, so that all trades show a paper loss to some extent. It is obvious that new positive information, such as a statement by the president of the central bank that the growth of the economy has increased more than expected, will be perceived as consonant. People will search the news for the least confirmation of the expected rise in interest rate. And worse, people will mutually reassure each other that they have interpreted the information correctly – a further addition of consonant cognition.

Remember that there are no friends in the financial markets, only the short-term community with shared solidarity of those who collectively will not admit to a loss.

The higher the dissonance, the greater the search for consonant information and the avoidance of dissonant news. However, this applies only up to a certain point. The selective quest for information may be halted if the dissonance is so high that there is no longer a prospect of it being reduced to a sufficiently low level. This could be the case if the loss has become so great that it is no longer acceptable to the trader and therefore a review of the original decision is imminent – he must liquidate his position and realize his loss. Paradoxically, this will result in a situation in which the actor no longer looks for information that confirms his original decision of buying US dollars against the euro. Rather, he needs information and opinions that justify the liquidation of his trade. News that was experienced earlier as dissonant is now consonant, while information perceived earlier as consonant is now experienced as dissonant in respect of the new decision.

In conclusion, we can analyze precisely how information is systematically distorted, and how information is sought and found that agrees with the current trade, following a trading decision, with the aid of cognitive dissonance theory. We may assume, for instance, that most players are in respect of the euro if they only ever comment positively on the development of the euro (as was the case at the start of 1990, when the euro was introduced). When these players suddenly start to quote negative news, it could be an indication that the majority has recently changed, or is changing, or intends to change its position as well as its opinion. These messages, which were previously deliberately overlooked, are now in great demand, so that the liquidation or the reversal of the trade is accompanied by as little dissonance as possible.

But the psyche of a market participant is not only liable to suffer dissonance after a decision. Many trading decisions are made after determining that they will give rise to as little dissonance as possible at a later stage. Naturally everybody assumes that their decisions will be profitable. The road to realization of these profits, however, may well be stony and paved with numerous small corrections and short-term losses. There will therefore be hardly a gain without moments of suffering (dissonance). The example of purchasing euros, after which the price rises continuously, leaving a big profit at the end is, unfortunately an exception.

A market participant will prefer certain instruments for his transactions (e.g. certain currencies) with which he has done well in the past, i.e. his trades were characterized by short-term dissonance only. The confirmation by a third party (naturally experienced as consonant) plays an important role. The inclination to buy dollars will not be particularly forceful once a trader's colleagues have informed him about the advantages of a short-term position and have "logically refuted" arguments in favor of buying. Who would depart from the norm set by his colleagues in that case? It may not be particularly opportune to take certain positions. Remember, for instance, the introduction of the euro in 1999, which was influenced radically by politicians and economists in all countries. On the other hand, one would not want to get involved with a currency that may have a good profit potential, but of which it is said that further development will be highly volatile.

The assimilation of information will be affected strongly even before the final decision not just by the anticipation of possible dissonance. In addition, there will usually be overconfidence in one's own skills and opportunities to influence events and the feeling of being able to control progress (overconfidence). Finally, one should always remember that the desire for control and minimization of dissonance will preferably be facilitated by the same means: matching information. This is usually easy to come by and cheap, in particular from those who are in the same situation.

It is therefore important to see whether, and how, information is assimilated by the majority of players. People often ask themselves why a particular piece of information, for instance positive economic data, or even a complete series of data, has not led to a upward movement of a currency or share, as might have been expected from a rational standpoint. In response, we might say that the new information was already incorporated in the price, i.e. traders had already traded and therefore there was no demand from their side immediately after publication of the data. Or the information did not agree with the trade, i.e. proceeding on the basis of this information would generate dissonance. It is therefore played down or even suppressed. Generally, however, it will not be passed on or even discussed with others, because in that case people would probably realize that they were holding a wrong position and, as a result, would have to do something.

EPILOGUE

If we consider once more the model introduced at the beginning, starting with the motive to enter a market up to the actual decision, then the role of information in the financial market becomes clear. The need to control the future and not be subject to dissonance, if at all possible, gives rise to selective perception, in addition to the natural physical limitations: the "right" information serves as a tranquilizer for the psyche. As information is processed differently, due to dissonance avoidance or loss aversion, winners may trade to a timescale different to losers: they realize their profits sooner and earlier. As a result, mostly losers remain in the market; they all experience the same damage limitation processes, as we have seen, and are therefore likely to trade simultaneously. And as they cannot always find sufficient counterparties immediately in order to liquidate their trades, prices will take off. This is how large trends are created.

So what is the main lesson to be drawn from all these findings? The most basic trading rule, namely to let profits run to a certain extent and to limit losses early, could be one answer. An experienced player might add that profits on average must be high enough to finance his transaction costs and to provide his earnings. But many readers will discover, even as early as the next trading day, that their psyche nevertheless copes better with many small profits and few losses, even though these are mostly large. They prefer one large operation to many small painful pinpricks, but most would prefer to celebrate many small successes, rather than one large one.

Readers who have merely become aware of the heuristics employed for processing information have already benefited, particularly if they are able to tell themselves that this time they have taken into account not only easily accessible information but also analyses and opinions that were difficult to obtain.

If people would only consider the actual consequences of their decisions in respect of future trades (irrespective of whether this concerns an act or an omission), it would also be a significant step in the direction of successful trading. Making rational decisions is the same as concentrating exclusively on the analysis of their consequences, without giving in to one's emotions and without glancing backwards. However, even Mrs Lot in the Old Testament did not manage to refrain from looking back.

The secret recipe sought by many, which supposedly will lead to profit time and time again, is discipline rather than forecast. The inscription at the temple in Delphi, "Know thyself", is therefore an important precondition. A computer model, which Ernest Coldheart should copy, may be the most important tool. But what use is perfect equipment if people lack the necessary discipline and switch it off? If every market participant possessed the necessary discipline, then this would mean a step in the direction of market efficiency, and Ernest Coldheart would have millions of like-minded brothers and sisters. The markets, however, would be boring, and the conversations soulless. Without fear there is no joy.

References

Abramson LY and Alloy LB (1980) Judgement of contingency: errors and their implication, in: Baum A and Singer E (eds) *Advances in Environmental Psychology*, Vol. 2, Hillsdale, Erlbaum.

Abramson LY, Seligman MEP and Teasdale JD (1978) Learned helplessness in humans: critique and reformulation, *Journal of Abnormal Psychology*, **37**, 49–74.

Anderson JR (1996) *Kognitive Psychologie – Eine Einführung*, 2nd edn, Heidelberg, Spektrum, Akademischer Verlag.

Antilla M (1977) *Consumer Price Perception*, Helsinki.

Aronson E (1994) *Sozialpsychologie: Menschliches Verhalten und gesellschaftlicher Einfluss*, Heidelberg, Spektrum, Akademischer Verlag.

Asch S (1946) Forming impressions of personality, *Journal of Abnormal and Social Psychology*, **41**, 258–90.

Auer-Rizzi W (1998) *Entscheidungprozesse in Gruppen: Kognitive und Soziale Verzerrungstendenzen*, Wiesbaden, Deutscher Universitätsverlag.

Beckmann J (1984) Kognitive Dissonanz, eine handlungstheoretische Perspektive, in: *Lehr- und Forschungstexte Psychologie* 11, Heidelberg, Springer-Verlag.

Beeler JD and Hunton J (1997) The influence of compensation method and disclosure level on information search strategy and escalation of commitment, *Journal of Behavioral Decision Making*, **10**, 77–91.

Benartzi S and Thaler RH (1995) Myopic loss aversion and the equity premium puzzle, *Quarterly Journal of Economics*, **10**, 73–92.

Bernoulli D (1738) Specimen theoriae novae de mensura sortis, *Commen. Acad. Sci. Imper. Petropolianae*, **5**, 175–92. Translated by Somer L (1954) *Econometrica*, **22**, 23–36.

Bernstein PL (1996) *Against the Gods: the remarkable story of risk*, New York, J. Wiley & Sons.

Bierhoff HW (1993) *Sozialpsychologie: ein Lehrbuch*, Stuttgart, Verlag W. Kohlhammer.

Bowman E (1980) A risk/return paradox for strategic management, *Sloan Management Review*, **21**(3), 17–31.

Bowman E (1982) Risk seeking by troubled firms, *Sloan Management Review*, **23**(4), 33–42.

Brehm JW (1956) Post-decision changes in the desirability of alternatives, *Journal of Abnormal and Social Psychology*, **52**, 384–9.

Brehm JW and Cohen AR (1962) *Explorations in Cognitive Dissonance*, New York, J. Wiley & Sons.

Brengelmann JC (1991) *Die Lust auf Spiel und Risiko*, Zurich, Varia Press.

Bruner JS and Postman L (1949–50) On the perception of incongruity: a paradigm, in: Bruner JS and Krech D (eds) *Perception and Personality: a symposium*, Durham, Duke University Press, 206–23.

Bungard W and Schulz-Gambard J (1990) Überlegungen zum Verhalten von Börsenakteuren aus kontrolltheoretischer Sicht, in: Maas P and Weibler J (eds) *Börse und Psychologie*, Cologne, Deutscher Instituts-Verlag, 140–61.

Camerer C and Weber M (1992) Recent developments in modelling preferences: uncertainty and ambiguity, *Journal of Risk and Uncertainty*, **5**, 325–70.

Christensen C (1989) The psychophysics of spending, *Journal of Behavioral Decision Making*, **2**, 69–80.

Dawes RM (1988) *Rational Choice in an Uncertain World*, Harcourt Brace Jovanovich, New York.

De Bondt WFM and Thaler RH (1985) Does the stock market overreact?, *Journal of Finance*, **40**(3), 793–805.

De Bondt WFM and Thaler RH (1995) Financial decision-making in markets and firms: a behavioral perspective, in: Jarrow R et al. (eds) *Handbooks in OR & MS*, Amsterdam, North Holland, 385–410.

DeCharms R (1968) *Personal Causation*, New York, Academic Press.

Dorsch F, Häcker H and Stapf KH (eds) (1994) *Dorsch, Psychologisches Wörterbuch*, 12th edn, Göttingen, Verlag Hans Huber.

Ehrlich D, Guttman J, Schonbach P and Mills J (1957) Postdecision exposure to relevant information, *Journal of Abnormal and Social Psychology*, **54**, 98–102.

Eisenführ F and Weber M (1999) *Rationales Entscheiden*, 3rd edn, Heidelberg, Springer-Verlag.

Elster J (1999) *Alchemies of the Mind: rationality and emotions*, Cambridge, Cambridge University Press.

Farquhar PH and Pratkanis AR (1993) Decision structuring with phantom alternatives, *Management Science*, **39**, 1214–26.

Fazio RH, Cooper M, Dayson K and Johnson M (1981) Control and the coronary-prone behavior pattern: responses to multiple situation demands, *Personality and Social Psychology Bulletin*, **7**, 97–102.

Felser G (1997) *Werbe- und Konsumentenpsychologie*, Heidelberg, Spektrum, Akademischer Verlag.

Festinger L (1957) *A Theory of Cognitive Dissonance*, Stanford, Stanford University Press.

Fiegenbaum A and Thomas H (1988) Attitudes towards risk and return and the risk–return paradox: prospect theory explanations, *Academy of Management Journal*, **38**, 85–106.

Fischhoff B (1975) Hindsight/foresight: the effect of outcome knowledge on judgment under uncertainty, *Journal of Experimental Psychology: Human Perception and Performance*, **1**, 288–99.

Fiske ST and Taylor SE (1991) *Social Cognition*, New York, McGraw Hill.

Folkerts-Landau D and Ito T (1995) *International Capital Markets, World Economic and Financial Surveys*, Washington, 165–74.

French K and Poterba JM (1991) Investor diversification and international equity markets, *American Economic Review, Papers and Proceedings*, **81**, 222–6.

Frey D (1976) Recent research on selective exposure to information, *Advances in Experimental Psychology*, **19**, 41–80.

Frey D (1981a) *Informationssuche und Informationsbewertung bei Entscheidungen*, Bern.

Frey D (1981b) Postdecisional preference for decision-relevant information as a function of the competence of its source and the degree of familiarity with this information, *Journal of Experimental Social Psychology*, **17**, 51–67.

Frey D and Gaska A (1998) Die Theorie der kognitiven Dissonanz, in: Frey D and Irle M (eds) *Theorien der Sozialpsychologie*, Vol. 1, 2nd edn, Bern, Verlag Hans Huber, 49–80.

Frey D and Schulz-Hardt S (1996) Eine Theorie der gelernten Sorglosigkeit, in: Mandl H (ed.) *Bericht über den 40. Kongress der Deutschen Gesellschaft für Psychologie in München 1996*, Göttingen, Hogrefe.

Frey D and Stahlberg D (1990) Erwartungsbildung und Erwartungsveränderungen bei Börsenakteuren, in: Maas P and Weibler J (eds) *Börse und Psychologie: Plädoyer für eine neue Perspektive*, Cologne, Deutscher Institutsverlag, 102–39.

Garber PM (1990) Who put the mania in the tulipmania?, in: White EM (ed.) *Crashes and Panics*, New York, Dow Jones Irwin, 33–56.

Gerke W and Bienert H (1993) Überprüfung des Dispositionseffektes und seiner Auswirkungen in computerisierten Börsenexperimenten, *Zeitschrift für betriebswirtschaftliche Forschung*, **31**, S169–94.

Glass DC and Singer J (1972) *Urban Stress*, New York, Academic Press.

Goethals GR, Cooper J and Naficy A (1979) Role of foreseen, foreseeable, and inforseeable behavioral consequences in the arousal of cognitive dissonance, *Journal of Personality and Social Psychology*, **37**, 1179–85.

Goldberg J (1990) *Erfolgreiche Devisenkursprognose: Handbuch der klassischen technischen Analyse für Devisenhandel, Aktienmärkte und Futures-Börsen*, Frankfurt, Verlag Börsen-Zeitung.

Goldberg J (1997) Behavioral Finance begründet Technische Analyse, *Börsenzeitung*, 28 November 1997.

Heath C and Tversky A (1991) Preference and belief: ambiguity and competence in choice under uncertainty, *Journal of Risk and Uncertainty*, **4**, 5–28.

Heller E (1995) *Wie Farben wirken*, Reinbek, Rowohlt Verlag.

Helson H (1964) *Adaptation Level Theory: an experimental and systematic approach to behavior*, New York, Harper and Row.

Herkner W (1980) *Attribution: Psychologie der Kausalität*, Bern, Huber.

Herrmann A and Bauer HH (1996) Ein Ansatz zur Preisbündelung auf der Basis der Prospect-Theorie, *Zeitschrift für betriebswirtschaftliche Forschung*, **48**, 675–94.

Higgins ET, Rholes WS and Jones CR (1977) Category accessibility and impression formation, *Journal of Experimental Social Psychology*, **13**, 141–54.

Hollenbeck JR, Ilgen DR, Philipps JM and Hedlund J (1994) Decision risk in dynamic two-stage contexts: beyond the status quo, *Journal of Applied Psychology*, **79**, 592–8.

Holler J (1996) *Das Neue Gehirn: Möglichkeiten moderner Hirnforschung*, Paderborn, Junfermannsche Verlagsbuchhandlung.

Hunter JE and Coggin DR (1988) Analyst judgment: the efficient market hypothesis versus a psychological theory of human judgment, *Organizational Behavior and Human Decision Processes*, **42**, 284–302.

Ibbotson RG and Ritter JR (1995) Initial public offerings, in: Jarrow R, Maksimovic V and Ziemba WT (eds) *Finance, Handbooks in Operations Research and Management Science*, Vol. 9, Amsterdam, North Holland, 993–1016.

Iyengar S and Kinder DR (1987) *News that Matters*, Chicago, University of Chicago Press.

Joseph R (1988) The neuropsychology of development: hemispheric laterality, limbic language, and the origin of thought, *Journal of Clinical Psychology*, **38**, 4–11.

Jungermann H, Pfister H-R and Fischer K (1998) *Die Psychologie der Entscheidung: Eine Einführung*, Heidelberg, Spektrum, Akademischer Verlag.

Kahneman D and Miller DT (1986) Norm theory: comparing reality to its alternatives, *Psychological Review*, **93**, 136–53.

Kahneman D, Slovic P and Tversky A (1982) *Judgment under Uncertainty: heuristics and biases*, New York, Cambridge University Press.

Kahneman D and Tversky A (1972) Subjective probability: a judgment of representativeness, *Cognitive Psychology*, **3**, 430–54.

Kahneman D and Tversky A (1973) On the psychology of prediction, *Psychological Review*, **80**, 237–51.

Kahneman D and Tversky A (1979) Prospect theory: an analysis of decision under risk, *Econometrica*, **47**, 263–91.

Kahneman D and Tversky A (1982a) Choices, values and frames, *American Psychologist*, **39**, 341–50.

Kahneman D and Tversky A (1982b The psychology of preferences, *Scientific American*, **146**, 160–73.

Keppe H-J (1997) *Ambiguität und Kompetenz*, Frankfurt, Peter Lang Verlag.

Kiell G and Stephan E (1997) Urteilsprozesse bei Finanzanlageentscheidungen von Experten. Abschlussbericht einer experimentellen Studie mit professionellen Devisenhändlern. Forschungsbericht des Instituts für Wirtschafts- und Sozialpsychologie der Universität Köln.

Kirchgässner G (1991) *Homo oeconomicus: das ökonomische Modell individuellen Verhaltens und seine Anwendung in den Wirtschafts- und Sozialwissenschaften*, Tübingen, JCB Mohr (Paw Siebeck).

Klix F (1976) *Information und Verhalten*, Bern, Huber.

Knetsch JL and Sinden JA (1984) Willingness to pay and compensation demanded: experimental evidence of an unexpected disparity in measures of value, *Quarterly Journal of Economics*, **99**, 507–21.

Langner EJ (1975) The illusion of control, *Journal of Personality and Social Psychology*, **32**, 311–28.

Levy SJ (1997) An introduction to prospect theory, in: Farnham B (ed.) *Avoiding Losses/Taking Risks*, 4th edn, Michigan, University of Michigan Press, 7–22.

Lichtenstein S, Fischhoff B and Phillips LD (1982) Calibration of probabilities: the state of the art to 1980, in: Kahneman D, Slovic P and Tversky A (eds) *Judgment under Uncertainty: heuristics and biases*, Cambridge, Cambridge University Press, 306–34.

Lichtenstein S and Slovic P (1971) Reversals of preference between bids and choices in gambling decisions, *Journal of Experimental Psychology*, **89**, 46–55.

Lichtenstein S, Slovic P, Fischhoff B, Layman M and Combs B (1978) Judged frequency of lethal events, *Journal of Experimental Psychology: Human Learning and Memory*, **4**, 551–78.

Lilli W and Frey D (1998) Die Hypothesentheorie der sozialen Wahrneh-mung, in: Frey D and Irle M (eds) *Theorien der Sozialpsychologie*, Vol. 1, 2nd edn, Bern, Verlag Hans Huber, 49–80.

Lim RG (1995) A range-frequency explanation of shifting reference points in risky decision making, *Organizational Behavior*, **63**, 6–20.

Linville PW and Fischer GW (1991) Attitudes and social cognition: preferences for separating or combining events, *Journal of Personality and Social Psychology*, **60**, 5–23.

Loewenstein G (1992) The fall and rise of psychological explanations in the economics of intemporal choice, in: Loewenstein G and Elter J (eds) *Choice over Time*, New York, Russell Sage Foundation, 3–34.

Loewenstein G and Thaler RH (1989) Anomalies: intertemporal choice, *Journal of Economic Perspectives*, **3**, 181–93.

Loomes G (1988) Further evidence of the impact of regret and dis-appointment in choice under uncertainty, *Econometrica*, **55**, 47–62.

Loomes G and Sugden R (1982) Regret theory: an alternative theory of rational choice under uncertainty, *Economic Journal*, **92**, 805–24.

Loomes G and Sugden R (1987) Testing for regret and disappointment in choice under uncertainty, *Economic Journal*, **97**, 118–29.

Maas P and Weibler J (1990a) Wahrnehmungs- und Informations-verarbeitungsprozesse an der Börse, in: Maas P and Weibler J (eds) *Börse und Psychologie: Plädoyer für eine neue Perspektive*, Cologne, Deutscher Institutsverlag, 72–101.

Maas P and Weibler J (1990b) Kontrollveränderungs- und Stress-reaktionen an der Börse, in: Maas P and Weibler J (eds) *Börse und Psychologie: Plädoyer für eine neue Perspektive*, Cologne, Deutscher Institutsverlag, 190–202.

MacLean PD (1977) The triune brain in conflict, *Psychotherapy and Psychosomatics*, **28**, 207–16.

MacLean PD (1978) A mind of three minds: educating the triune brain, in: *Education and the Brain, the Seventy-seventh Yearbook of the National Society for the Study of Education*, Part II, Chicago, University of Chicago Press, 308–42.

MacLean PD (1983) Brain roots of the will-to-power, *Zygon*, **18**, 359–74.

MacLean PD (1985) Evolutionary psychiatry and the triune brain, *Psychological Medicine*, **15**, 219–22.

MacLean PD (1990) *The Triune Brain in Evolution: role in paleocerebral functions*, New York, Plenum Press.

MacLean PD (1993) Cerebral evolution of emotions, in: Lewis M and Haviland JM (eds) *Handbook of Emotions*, New York, Guildford Press, 67–83.

Maital S (1986) What do people bring to the stock market (besides money)? The economic psychology of stock market behavior, in: Gilad B and Kaish S (eds) *Handbook of Behavioral Economics*, Vol. B, London, JAI Press, 273–307.

Mann L (1994) *Sozialpsychologie*, 10th edn, Weinheim, Psychologie Verlagsunion.

March JG and Sharpira Z (1987) Managerial perspectives on risk taking, *Management Science*, **33**, 1404–17.

Markowitz HG (1952) Portfolio (Selection), *Journal of Finance*, **7**, 77–91.

Markowitz HM (1959) *Portfolio (Selection), Efficient Diversification of Investments*, New York, J. Wiley & Sons.

Medea A and Thompson K (1974) *Against Rape*, New York, Farrar, Straus and Giroux.

Meyer W-U and Försterling F (1998) Die Attributionstheorie, in: Frey D and Irle M (eds) *Theorien der Sozialpsychologie*, Vol. 1, 2nd edn, Bern, Verlag Hans Huber, 175–216.

Miller GA (1956) The magical number seven, plus or minus two: some limits on our capacity for processing information, *Psychological Review*, **63**, 81–97.

Miller IW and Norman WH (1979) Learned helplessness in humans: a review and attribution theory model, *Psychological Bulletin*, **86**, 93–118.

Neal LD (1990) How the South Sea Bubble was blown up and burst, in: White EN (ed.) *Crashes and Panics*, New York, Dow Jones Irwin, 33–56.

Nisbett RE (1976) Popular induction: information is not always informative, in: Carrol JS and Payne JW (eds) *Cognition and Social Behavior*, Hillsdale, Erlbaum, 227–36.

Nwokoye NG (1975) Subjective judgements of price: the effect of price parameters on adaption levels, in: Mazze EM (ed.) *Combined Proceedings of AMA*, 545–8.

Oberlechner R and Hocking S (1997) *Market Psychology and the Dynamics of Information, An Interdisciplinary View of the Foreign Exchange Market*, Vienna, Webster University.

Oehler A (1998) Abnehmende oder zunehmende relative Risikoaversion?, *Zeitschrift für Bankrecht und Bankwirtschaft*, **10**, 230–6.

Osnabrügge G, Stahlberg D and Frey D (1998) Die Theorie der kognizierten Kontrolle, in: Frey D and Irle M (eds) *Theorien der Sozialpsychologie*, Vol. 3, Bern, Verlag Hans Huber, 127–74.

Perkins CC Jr (1968) An analysis of the concept of reinforcement, *Psychological Review*, **75**, 155–72.

Pratkanis AR, Farquhar PH, Silbert S and Hearst J (1989) *Decoys Produce Contrast Effects and Alter Choice Probabilities*, Santa Cruz.

Pyszczynski TA and Greenberg J (1987) Toward an integration of cognitive and motivational perspectives on social inference: a biased hypothesis-testing model, in: Berkowitz L (ed.) *Advances in Experimental Social Psychology*, San Diego.

Qualls WJ and Puto CP (1989) Organizational climate and decision framing: an integrated approach to analyzing industrial buying decisions, *Journal of Marketing Research*, **26**, 179–92.

Rapp HW (1997) "Der tägliche Wahnsinn hat Methode" – Behavioral Finance: Paradigmenwechsel in der Kaptialmarktforschung, in: Jünemann B and Schellenberger D (eds) *Psychologie für Börsenprofis*, Stuttgart, Verlag Schäffer-Poeschel.

Rescher N (1993) *Rationalität, Eine philosophische Untersuchung über das Wesen und die Begründung der Venunft*, Würzburg, Verlag Königshausen & Neumann.

Roelofsma PHMP and Keren G (1995) Framing and time-inconsistent preferences, in: Caverni J-P, Bar-Hillel M, Hutton Baron M and Jungermann H (eds) *Contribution to Decision Making*, Amsterdam, Elsevier Science, 351–61.

Ross L (1977) The intuitive psychologist and his shortcomings: distortions in the attribution process, in: Berkowitz L (ed.) *Advances in Experimental Social Psychology*, New York, Academic Press, 173–220.

Rothbaum F, Weisz JR and Snyder SS (1982) Changing the world and changing the self: a two-process model of perceived control, *Journal of Personality and Social Psychology*, **42**, 5–37.

Rotter JB (1966) Generalized expectations for internal vs. external control of reinforcement, *Psychological Monographs*, **80**, 1–28.

Samuelson P (1963) Risk and uncertainty: a fallacy of large numbers, *Scientia*, **78**, 108–13.

Samuelson W and Zeckhauser R (1988) Status quo bias in decision making, *Journal of Risk and Uncertainty*, **1**, 7–59.

Sauer C and Müller M (1980) Die Theorie der gelernten Hilflosigkeit: Eine hilfreiche Theorie?, *Zeitschrift für Sozialpsychologie*, **11**, 2–25.

Schachter S, Hood DC, Andreassen PB and Gerin W (1986) Aggregate variables in psychology and economics: dependence and the stock market, in: Gilad B and Kaish S (eds) *Handbook of Behavioral Economics*, Part B, Vol. 2, Greenwich, 237–71.

Schulz R and Aderman D (1973) Effect of residential change on temporal distance to death of terminal cancer patients, *Journal of Death and Dying*, **4**, 157–62.

Schulz-Hardt S, Frey D and Lüthgens C (1996) Sorglosigkeit und risikoakzeptanz, in: Wenninger G and Graf Hoyos C (eds) *Arbeits-, Gesundheits- und Umweltschutz*, Heidelberg, Asanger, 468–79.

Schwartz H (1998) *Rationality Gone Awry? Decision making inconsistent with economic and financial theory*, Westport, Praeger Publishers.

Schwarz N and Bohner G (1990) Stimmungseinflüsse auf Denken und Entscheiden, in: Maas P and Weibler J (eds) *Börse und Psychologie: Plädoyer für eine neue Perspektive*, Cologne, Deutscher Institutsverlag, 162–89.

Seligman MEP (1975) *Helplessness: on depression, development, and death*, San Francisco, Harvard University Press.

Sharpe WE (1970) *Theory and Capital Markets*, New York, McGraw-Hill.

Shefrin H and Statman M (1985) The disposition to sell winners too early and ride losers too long: theory and evidence, *Journal of Finance*, **40**, 777–92.

Simon HA (1955) A behavioral model of rational choice, *Quarterly Journal of Economics*, **69**, 99–118.

Simon HA (1997) *Models of Bounded Rationaliy, Empirically Grounded Economic Reason*, 2nd edn, Cambridge, MIT Press.

Sklar LS and Anisman H (1981) Stress and cancer, *Psychological Bulletin*, **89**, 369–406.

Slovic P, Griffin D and Tversky A (1990) Compatibility effects in judgement and choice, in: Hogarth R (ed.) *Insights in Decision Making: a tribute to Hillel J. Einhorn*, Chicago, University of Chicago Press, 5–27.

Stahlberg D, Osnabrügge G and Frey D (1998) Die Theorie der kognizierten Kontrolle, in: Frey D and Irle M (eds) *Theorien der Sozialpsychologie*, Vol. 3, Bern, Verlag Hans Huber, 79–124.

Stephan E (1999) Die Rolle von Urteilsheuristiken bei Finanzentscheidungen: Ankereffekte und kognitive Verfügbarkeit, in: Fischer L, Kutsch T and Stephan E (eds) *Finanzpsychologie*, Munich, Verlag R. Ouldenburg.

Strack F (1998) Urteilsheuristiken, in: Frey D and Irle M (eds) *Theorien der Sozialpsychologie*, Vol. 3, Bern, Verlag Hans Huber, 239–68.

Thaler RH (1980) Toward a positive theory of consumer choice, *Journal of Economic Behavior and Organization*, **1**, 39–60.

Thaler RH (1985) Mental accounting and consumer choice, *Marketing Science*, **4**, 199–214.

Thaler RH (1994) *Quasi Rational Economics*, New York, Russell Sage Foundation.

Thaler RH and Johnson EJ (1990) Gambling with the house money and trying to break even: the effects of prior outcomes on risky choice, *Management Science*, **36**, 643–60.

Thompson SC (1981) Will it hurt if I can control it? A complex answer to a simple question, *Psychological Bulletin*, **90**, 89–101.

Tversky A and Kahneman D (1974) Judgement under uncertainty: heuristics and biases, *Science*, **185**, 1124–31.

Tversky A and Kahneman D (1981) The framing of decisions and the psychology of choice, *Science*, **22**, 453–8.

Tversky A and Kahneman D (1983) Extensional versus intuitive reasoning: the conjunction fallacy in probability judgement, *Psychological Review*, **90**, 293–315.

Tversky A and Kahneman D (1986) Rational choice and the framing of decisions, *Journal of Business*, **59**, 251–78.

Tversky A and Kahneman D (1991) Loss aversion and riskless choice: a reference dependent model, *Quarterly Journal of Economics*, **6**, 1039–61.

Tversky A and Kahneman D (1992) Advances in prospect theory, *Journal of Risk and Uncertainty*, **5**, 297–323.

Tversky A, Slovic P and Kahneman D (1990) The causes of preference reversal, *American Economic Review*, **80**, 204–17.

Vroon P (1993) *Drei Hirne im Kopf*, Zurich, Kreuz Verlag AG.

Von Nitzsch R (1998a) Prospect Theory und Käuferverhalten, *Die Betriebswirtschaft*, **58**, 621–34.

Von Nitzsch R (1998b) *Entscheidungslehre, "Der Weg zu besseren Entscheidung"*, 3rd edn, Aachen.

Von Nitzsch R and Friedrich C (1999) *Entscheidungen in Finanzmärkten, "Psychologische Grundlagen"*, Aachen, Augustinus Verlag Aachen.

Weber M (1993) Besitztumseffekte: eine theoretische und experimentelle Analyse, *Die Betriebswirtschaft*, **53**, 479–90.

Weber M and Camerer C (1998) The disposition effect in securities trading: an experimental analysis, *Journal of Economic Behavior and Organization*, **33**, 167–84.

White RW (1959) Motivation reconsidered: the concept of competence, *Psychological Review*, **66**, 297–333.

Wicklund RA and Brehm JW (1976) *Perspectives on Cognitive Dissonance*, Hillsdale, Erlbaum.

Wiswede G (1995) *Einführung in die Wirtschaftspsychologie*, Munich, Ernst Reinhardt Verlag.

Wyer RS Jr and Srull RK (1980) The processing of social stimulus information: a conceptual integration, in: Hastie R, Ostrom TM, Ebbesen EB, Wyer RS, Hamilton D and Carlston DE (eds) *Person Memory: the cognitive basis of social perception*, Hillsdale, Erlbaum.

Yaniv I and Foster DP (1997) Precision and accuracy of judgmental estimation, *Journal of Behavioral Decision Making*, **10**, 21–32.

Zimbardo PG (1965) The effect of effort and improvisation on self-persuasion produced by role-playing, *Journal of Experimental Social Psychology*, **1**, 103–20.
Zimbardo PG (1995) *Psychologie*, 6th edn, Berlin, Springer.

Further reading

Albin PS (1998) *Barriers and Bounds to Rationality: essays on economic complexity and dynamics in interactive systems*, Princeton, Princeton University Press.

Anderson BF and Settle JW (1996) The influence of portfolio characteristics and investment period on investment choice, *Journal of Economic Psychology*, **17**, 343–58.

Arkes HR (1996) The psychology of waste, *Journal of Behavioral Decision Making*, **9**, 213–24.

Arkes HR and Blumer C (1985) The psychology of sunk cost, *Organizational Behavior and Human Decision Processes*, **35**, 124–40.

Belsky G and Gilovich T (1999) *Why Smart People Make Big Money Mistakes*, New York, Simon & Schuster.

Busch F (1999) *Greife nie in ein fallendes Messer*, Frankfurt, Campus Verlag.

Currim IS and Sarin RK (1989) Prospect versus utility, *Management Science*, **35**, 22–41.

De Bondt WFM and Thaler RH (1980) Do security analysts overreact?, *AEA Papers and proceedings*, **80**, 52–7.

Dörner D (1989) *The Logic of Failure: why things go wrong and what we can do to make them right*, Metropolitan Books, New York.

Fischer K (1997), *Tun oder Lassen? Die Rolle von framing-Prozessen für die Wahl von Handlungen oder Unterlassung in Entscheidungssituationen*, Frankfurt, Lang.

Fischer L and Wiswede G (1997) *Grundlagen der Sozialpsychologie*, Munich, Ouldenbourg.

Frey D and Irle M (eds) (1993a) *Theorien der Sozialpsychologie*, Vol. I: Kognitive theorien, 2nd edn, Bern, Verlag Hans Huber.

Frey D and Irle M (eds) (1993b) *Theorien der Sozialpsychologie*, Vol. II: Gruppen- und Lerntheorien, 2nd edn, Bern, Verlag Hans Huber.

Friedman M and Rosenman RH (1974) *Type A Behavior and Your Heart*, New York, Knopf.

Geweke J (ed.) (1992) *Decision Making under Risk and Uncertainty*, Dordrecht, Kluwer Academic Publishers.

Gilovich R (1993) *How We Know What Isn't So: the fallibility of human reason in everyday life*, New York, Free Press.

Goldstein WM and Hogarth RM (1997) *Research on Judgment and Decision Making: currents, connections and controversies*, Cambridge, Cambridge University Press.

Green L and Kagel JH (eds) (1990) *Advances in Behavioral Economics*, 2nd edn, Norwood, Ablex Publishing.

Gross L (1982) *The Art of Selling Intangibles: How to Make your Million ($) by Investing Other People's Money*, New York, Prentice Hall.

Haugen RA (1995) *The New Finance: the case against efficient markets*, Engelwood Cliffs, Prentice Hall.

Haugen RA (1997) *Modern Investment Theory*, 4th edn, Engelwood Cliffs, Prentice Hall.

Hell W, Fiedler K and Gigerenzer G (1993) *Kognitive Täuschungen*, Heidelberg, Spektrum Akademischer Verlag.

Izard CE (1995) *Die Emotionen des Menschen: Eine Einführung in die Grundlagen der Emotionspsychologie*, 3rd edn, Weinheim, Beltz.

Janis IL (1982) *Groupthink: psychological studies of policy decisions and fiascos*, Boston, Houghton Mifflin.

Jünemann B and Schellenberger D (eds) (1997) *Psychologie für Börsenprofis*, Stuttgart, Verlag Schäffer-Poeschel.

Kahneman D, Knetsch JG and Thaler RG (1991) The endowment effect, loss aversion and status quo bias, *Journal of Economic Perspectives*, **5**, 193–206.

Kahneman D and Slovic P (eds) (1982) *Judgment under Uncertainty*, New York, Cambridge University Press.

Kaish S and Gilad B (eds) (1991) *Handbook of Behavioral Economics*, 2nd edn: Behavioral Environments, Greenwich, JAI Press.

Koppel R and Abell H (1994) *The Inner Game of Trading: modelling the psychology of the top performing traders*, Chicago, Probus Publishing.

Loewenstein G and Elster J (eds) (1992) *Choice over Time*, New York, Russell Sage Foundation.

Lüthi AFJ (1993) *Massenpsychologie im Devisenhandel, Swiss Banking School*, Vol. 75, Bern, Verlag Paul Haupt.

Maital S (1982) *Minds, Markets and Money: psychological foundations of economic behavior*, New York, Basic Books.

Markowitsch HJ (ed.) (1988) *Information Processing by the Brain*, Toronto, Hans Huber.

Menkhoff L (1995) *Spekulative Verhaltensweisen auf Devisenmärkten*, Tübingen, CB Mohr (Paul Siebeck).

Murphy JJ (1986) *Technical Analysis of the Futures Markets*, New York, New York Institute of Finance.

Nisbett R and Ross L (1980) *Human Inference: strategies and shortcomings of social judgment*, Engelwood Cliffs, Prentice Hall.

Oehler A (1992) "Anomalien", "Irrationalitäten" oder "Biases" der Erwartungsnutzentheorie und Ihre Relevanz für die Finanzmärkte, *Zeitschrift für Bankrecht und Bankwirtschaft*, 4, 97–124.

Pinner W (1997) *Die verrückte Börse: Eine Einführung in die Börsenpsychologie*, Düsseldorf, ECON Verlag.

Plous S (1993) *The Psychology of Judgement and Decision Making*, New York, McGraw-Hill.

Plummer T (1990) *The Psychology of Technical Analysis*, Chicago, Probus Publishing.

Restak RM (1989) *Geheimnisse des menschlichen Gehirns*, Landsberg, MVG-Verlag.

Roth G (1996) *Das Gehirn und seine Wirklichkeit*, 5th edn, Frankfurt, Auflage.

Russo EJ and Schoemaker PJ (1990) *Decision Traps: ten barriers to brilliant decision-making and how to overcome them*, New York, Fireside.

Schachter S and Gazzaniga MS (eds) (1989) *Extending Psychological Frontiers: selected works of Leon Festinger*, New York, Russell Sage Foundation.

Schulz-Hardt S (1997) *Realitätsflucht in Entscheidungsprozessen: vom Groupthink zum Entscheidungsautismus*, Bern, Verlag Hans Huber.

Schwarz N (1982) Homo Heuristicus: Zur Psychologie des kognitiven Geizhalses, *Zeitschrift für Sozialpsychologie*, 13, 343–7.

Sen A (1997) *Choice, Welfare and Measurement*, Oxford, Harvard University Press.

Shefrin HM and Statman M (1984) Explaining investor preference for cash dividends, *Journal of Financial Economics*, 13, 253–82.

Thaler R (1987) *The Psychology of Choice and the Assumptions of Economics*, Maryland, University of Maryland.

Thaler RH (1993) *Advances in Behavioral Finance*, New York, Russell Sage Foundation.

Tversky A and Thaler RH (1990) Anomalies-preference reversals, *Journal of Economics Perspectives*, 4, 201–11.

Unser M (1999) *Behavioral Finance am Aktienmarkt, Empirische Analysen zum Risikoverhalten individueller Anleger*, Bad Soden, Uhlenbruch Verlag.

Weber M (1989) Ambiguität in Finanz- und Kapitalmärkten, *Zeitschrift für betriebswirtschaftliche Forschung*, 41, 447–71.

White EN (ed.) (1990) *Crashes and Panics: the lessons from history*, Homewood, Dow Jones Irwin.

Wood AS (ed.) (1995) *Behavioral Finance and Decision Theory in*

Investment Management, Charlottesville, Association for Investment Management and Research.

Zimbardo PG and Gerrig RJ (1999) *Psychologie*, 7th edn, Berlin, Springer Verlag.

Index